2 Writing Projects

Practical lessons based on classical methods

Brian Moon

chalkface

First published in Australia 2011

Chalkface Press P/L
PO Box 23
Cottesloe WA 6011 AUSTRALIA

www.chalkface.net.au

Designed by Alexa Koch and Stephen Mellor
Edited by Bronwyn Mellor

National Library of Australia Cataloguing-in-Publication entry

Moon, Brian, 1958-
Writing projects 2 : practical lessons based on classical
methods / by Brian Moon ; edited by Bronwyn Mellor.

ISBN 9781875136308 (pbk.)
Includes index.

For secondary school age.
Writing--Study and teaching (Secondary)
Creative writing.
English language--Rhetoric.

Mellor, Bronwyn.

808.0688

Printed in Western Australia by Lamb Print, Perth, WA 6021 on 'ENVI Laser' paper made from elemental chlorine-free pulp derived from sustainably managed forests and non-controversial sources. It is certified carbon neutral under Australian ISO 14001 certification, which guarantees use of renewable energy sources.

Contents

Acknowledgements

This book was made possible by a grant of study leave from Edith Cowan University, for which I am extremely grateful. I thank Professor Greg Robson, Dr Tim McDonald and members of the Faculty of Education and Arts grants committee for their support in helping me secure the time to work on the project.

I particularly thank my colleagues, Mrs Barbara Harris, for generously taking on extra teaching and administration during my absence, and Mrs Julie Keane, for stepping into the breach to help cover my classes. Their hard work enabled me to enjoy the guilty pleasure of spending an entire semester writing about writing. Thanks are due also to my students at ECU, who have helped me to refine my thinking and teaching about the business of writing.

As always, Bronwyn Mellor at Chalkface Press has provided invaluable editorial advice, saving me from any number of conceptual, stylistic and organisational errors. Needless to say, whatever errors or inconsistencies remain are mine.

Personal thanks go to Stephen Nichols for many enjoyable and sustaining discussions about writing, literature and aeroplanes.

Finally, I thank my wife, Annette, without whose patience and support the project could not have been completed.

Sources

Project 1: Charles Dickens, from *Bleak House* (1853), Penguin, Harmondsworth, 1971.

Project 2: Pär Lagerkvist, "Father and I", from *The Marriage Feast and Other Stories*, trans. Alan Blair, London: Chatto & Windus, 1955.

Project 3: Michel de Montaigne, "On Liars", from *Essays* (1580). Translated by J.M. Cohen. Harmondsworth: Penguin, 1958. Abridged and adapted for the present volume.

Project 4: Prime Minister Kevin Rudd. "Apology to Australia's Indigenous Peoples", *House of Representatives Official Hansard,* No.1, 2008. Commonwealth of Australia. 167–73. Wednesday, February 13, 2008. From http://www.aph.gov.au/hansard. Abridged.

The recording sheets for analysing style (pages 147–151) have been adapted from Corbett, E.P.J. & Connors, R.J. (1999). *Classical Rhetoric for the Modern Student*. 4th ed. New York: Oxford UP. Usage of the various rhetorical terms follows the guidelines in Lanham, R.A. (1991). *A Handlist of Rhetorical Terms*. 2nd ed. Berkeley: University of California Press. References to the various classical treatises are taken from Bizzell, P. & Herzberg, B. (Eds). (2001). *The Rhetorical Tradition: Readings from Classical Times to the Present*. 2nd ed. Boston: Bedford/ St Martin's. English language definitions and etymologies are based on *The Shorter Oxford English Dictionary* (2002). 5th ed. Oxford University Press.

To the teacher

Writing Projects offers a radical approach to writing instruction. Drawing on the techniques of classical rhetoric, the series teaches writing through a collection of practical projects, from single-sentence proverbs to complex descriptions, stories, essays and more.

This second volume teaches advanced techniques in narrative, description and exposition. It covers the use of theme, motif and symbol; selection and presentation of detail in narrative; argument and proof, through reason, evidence and authority; and techniques for appealing to an audience. Students will also learn a range of new technical terms, from *apomnemonysis* to *prosopopoeia*. These important and challenging skills are taught through description, short story, essay and speech writing.

Each project offers comprehensive, step-by-step instructions for a complete writing task, leading students from reading and analysis to composition. The chapters incorporate a range of specialised strategies, including dictation, imitations, extensions, and practice exercises.

The content of each project includes:

- ■ models of effective writing by established authors
- ■ discussions of use and purpose that put the writing in context
- ■ practice exercises to teach skills of diction, sentencing and figurative style
- ■ marking guides to assist assessment and self-assessment
- ■ quizzes and tests to build knowledge about writers, terms and styles

The learning is activity-based, with suggested answers for each task supplied at the end of the project. The individual chapters can serve, therefore, as fully planned lessons for the classroom, or as independent study packages.

A word about the method

Writing Projects applies the techniques of a classical training system for teaching writing. All the methods used in the projects have been derived from research into the system of *rhetoric* – a discipline first codified by scholars around 500 BC. Along with grammar and logic, rhetoric has been a cornerstone of classical education for around two thousand years. It has produced some of the greatest writers and orators in Western literature, including Shakespeare, whose plays and poems reveal the rhetorical skills he acquired as a schoolboy.

Like the training systems on which it is modelled, *Writing Projects* makes careful use of imitative writing and copying tasks. The approach may seem alien to modern teachers, who fear that imitation will stifle students' creativity. Yet copying and imitation are powerful forms of learning. Classical scholars used imitation to teach their students concentration and correctness, laying a foundation of technical skill in preparation for subsequent invention.

More so than their counterparts in earlier times, modern students may have limited exposure to formal and literary uses of language. In daily life they use the abbreviated forms associated with modern technology. Imitating the styles and techniques of accomplished writers helps students learn the patterns and rhythms of literary language through conscious attention to structure, sentence forms, word choice, and punctuation. That learning will serve them well as they go on to develop their own personal styles.

Teachers who want to know more about classical instruction and rhetoric will find the following references a useful starting point for study.

Bizzell, P. & Herzberg, B. (Eds). (2001). *The Rhetorical Tradition: Readings from Classical Times to the Present.* Boston: Bedford/St Martin's.

Corbett, E.P.J. & Connors, R.J. (Eds). (1999). *Classical Rhetoric for the Modern Student.* (4th ed.). New York: Oxford University Press.

Golden, J.L. & Corbett, E.P.J. (Eds). (1990). *The Rhetoric of Blair, Campbell and Whateley.* Carbondale: Southern Illinois UP.

Lanham, R.A. (1991). *A Handlist of Rhetorical Terms.* (2nd ed.). Berkeley: University of California Press.

Brian Moon is a senior lecturer in the School of Education at Edith Cowan University in Perth, Western Australia. He is the author of *Viewing Terms: A Practical Glossary for Film and TV Study; Literary Terms: A Practical Glossary; Studying Poetry; Studying Literature;* and is co-author of *Writing Critical Essays: A Practical Guide,* all published by Chalkface Press.

To the student

The art of rhetoric: writing with style

Around 500 BC, the Ancient Greeks developed a set of rules for successful writing and public speaking. They studied the techniques of the best writers and speakers, and discovered the most effective ways to argue a point, or stir an emotion, or paint a picture, using nothing but words and voice. Their findings became the foundation for the great art of *rhetoric* – the art of effective communication.

Many of the early Greek experts in rhetoric became famous for their skill with words. Calling themselves *sophists* (wise men), they travelled the country demonstrating their skills at public gatherings. They would speak without rehearsal on any topic the audience threw at them, and they defeated their opponents with clever arguments and flashes of style. After their demonstrations they would offer lessons to anyone prepared to pay. Because public speaking was so important in Greek society, they had no shortage of students. One of the sophists, a man named Gorgias, became so wealthy from the fees paid by his students that he had a gold statue of himself erected at a temple in his home city.

Later, around 350 BC, the philosopher Aristotle expanded the principles of rhetoric and wrote them down in a single book, which he called *The Art of Rhetoric*. Aristotle frowned on the early sophists like Gorgias, who he believed were more interested in making money than seeking the truth. But he recognised and built upon their discoveries. The proper use of rhetoric, Aristotle said, was to help improve humanity by improving the quality of public discussion and communication. His book not only taught readers how to win arguments through persuasive writing and speech; it also included advice on clear expression, logical thinking, and ethics. *The Art of Rhetoric* became one of the most influential books ever written. For around two thousand years it served as a blueprint for training students in the skills of public speaking and writing.

For many centuries the study of rhetoric was considered essential to a good education. Anyone involved in government, the law, education, or public service, was trained in Aristotle's rules. From classical times, through the Middle Ages, and into the early modern period, the study of rhetoric flourished. Many of the greatest English writers, including Shakespeare, learned their craft from Aristotle's famous book, or from new books written especially for the schools that began to spring up in the 16th century. In our modern schools, however, the study of rhetoric has largely disappeared, and the ancient knowledge has been all but lost.

This book revives some of the ancient principles of rhetorical training. Its aim is to restore some of the lost knowledge and provide a solid foundation for the study of writing techniques and styles.

How does it work?

Nowadays we tend to think of writing as a mysterious and magical creative process, something that cannot be taught – but that is a new and rather odd idea. For many centuries writing was looked upon as a practical skill that could be taught and learned, just as we now teach skills like playing tennis or driving a car.

The ancient teachers of rhetoric had a straightforward system for teaching writing. There were two main methods: *reading and imitating the work of experts*, and *learning the rules and skills* for specific tasks. It was a practical system. Just as we might learn to play tennis by watching top players and copying their action, so the students of rhetoric copied the styles of successful writers. Just as we might work on our racquet skills, so the students of rhetoric worked on their word skills. After acquiring different techniques from each writer they studied, the students would develop styles of their own.

Like the ancient schoolbooks, this text is based on imitation, rules, and skills. Each project in the book starts with an example by a successful writer. Your task is to write an imitation of that original piece. The examples have been chosen to highlight particular designs and features of style. As you work through the different projects, you will learn the rules to follow and the skills to use in your writing. Eventually, you will develop a style of your own.

Although the method is simple to describe, you will soon discover that copying what the experts can do is not easy. Imitation is a powerful form of learning; but it requires close attention to detail, accuracy, and practice. The rules and skills need careful study, too. You wouldn't expect to excel in your favourite sport without training, and learning to write well is no different.

There are five main steps in each project. You will need to follow the steps closely and complete the activities in each one. Everything you need to complete each project is included. That includes ideas, plans and starting points for your writing. The instructions for each task are very detailed. You will never be left staring at a blank page wondering what to do. Provided you put in the effort and follow the steps, you will learn and succeed.

Some final tips

In some projects there are new terms to learn, including special names for the rules and skills you will meet. You should keep a list of these new terms in a section of your notebook or file. Make sure you learn the meaning and the spelling of each.

There are marking keys and quizzes at the end of each project. Keep this in mind as you work through the activities. You will score better by remembering what you read and by imitating the original work as closely as possible. Once you have completed the project you will be ready to try more creative activities in the section titled "Going further".

Copying the writing of experts is a great way to learn, but remember, you should never publish these pieces as your own original work. If you are called on to display your work, you must acknowledge the original writer. Here are two examples that show how to do it.

An essay: "On Friendship" by Lucy Tyler. *(Based upon the essay "On Liars" by Michel de Montaigne, 1580.)*

A short story: "Mother and I" by Kareem Abujani. *(Adapted from the short story "Father and I" by Pär Lagerkvist, 1955.)*

Finally – some of the projects require you to do some simple maths. If you struggle with mental arithmetic, you might find a calculator helpful for those sections.

The Project Steps

EACH CHAPTER FOLLOWS THIS FIVE-STEP PATTERN

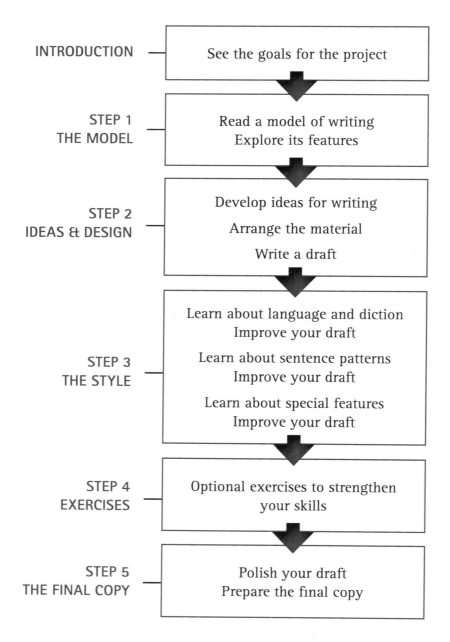

INTRODUCTION — See the goals for the project

STEP 1
THE MODEL — Read a model of writing
Explore its features

STEP 2
IDEAS & DESIGN — Develop ideas for writing
Arrange the material
Write a draft

STEP 3
THE STYLE — Learn about language and diction
Improve your draft

Learn about sentence patterns
Improve your draft

Learn about special features
Improve your draft

STEP 4
EXERCISES — Optional exercises to strengthen
your skills

STEP 5
THE FINAL COPY — Polish your draft
Prepare the final copy

Project 1: Write a description

Introduction

IN THIS SECTION:
■ Preview the task

A description is a written impression of a person, place or thing. The word "describe" comes from the Latin verb *scribere*, and means simply "to write down" or record in words. Writing a description, then, is like taking a photograph with words instead of light.

The types of description are limitless. Descriptions can be short or long. They can be dry and factual or rich, imaginative and stylish. But all descriptions must do essentially the same thing: they must present the key features of the thing being described, and record them in a way that will have some impact on the reader.

In this project you will learn how to create a written impression of a place. Learning to write effective description will help you to develop important skills. You will learn to select and organise details, arrange the material, develop a theme, and write in a style that will help your reader visualise something that he or she may never have seen.

Goal: Write a description that presents a powerful impression of a time and place.

Skills you will learn from this project:

■ selecting details using rules of *number, variety, scale* and *degree*
■ arranging the material in a literary *frame*
■ using descriptive techniques of *comparison, personification, anachronism*
■ using new sentence styles: *fragments, compounds, repetitions*

Special terms: *anaphora, anachronism, prosopopoeia*

Step 1: The model

IN THIS SECTION:
- Read an example
- Explore its features and usage

For this project you will copy a famous description by one of the most successful English writers of all time, Charles Dickens (1812–1870). Dickens worked as a reporter in law courts and in the newspaper industry before moving on to write serial stories, pamphlets and novels. His earliest works were published in London's *Morning Chronicle* newspaper under the pen name of "Boz". His novels were written and published in monthly instalments that sold for a shilling each. Among his most famous works are *Oliver Twist* (1838), *David Copperfield* (1850), and *Great Expectations* (1861).

Before reading

On the next page is a passage from one of Dickens' most respected novels, *Bleak House* (1853). In the passage, Dickens describes the city of London in winter, around 1852. *Bleak House* is about a long-running legal case. In his description, Dickens makes a number of references to the courts and the Lord Chancellor, which are the subjects of the novel. Also mentioned are some of the districts and landmarks around the city.

Read the passage carefully, paying attention to the *descriptions of mud and fog*. This is the model you will copy in your own writing.

Words to know:

> *Michaelmas Term* – the university term that begins in September
>
> *Chancery* – the Lord Chancellor's court
>
> *Lincoln's Inn Hall* – the location of the Chancery court
>
> *Ait* – a small island in a river
>
> *Collier-brig* – a small ship that transports coal
>
> *Husbandman* – a farmer
>
> *Wonderful (in the context "...not be wonderful to meet...")* – surprising
>
> *Megalosaurus ("great lizard")* – a type of large meat-eating theropod (running on hind legs) dinosaur of the middle Jurassic period of 166 million years ago in Europe.

Bleak House

1 London. Michaelmas term lately over, and the Lord Chancellor sitting in Lincoln's Inn Hall. Implacable November weather. As much mud in the streets as if the waters had but newly retired from the face of the earth, and it would not be wonderful to meet a Megalosaurus, forty feet long or so, waddling like an elephantine lizard up Holborn Hill. Smoke lowering
5 down from chimney-pots, making a soft black drizzle, with flakes of soot in it as big as full-grown snowflakes – gone into mourning, one might imagine, for the death of the sun. Dogs, undistinguishable in mire. Horses, scarcely better; splashed to their very blinkers. Foot passengers, jostling one another's umbrellas in a general infection of ill temper, and losing their foot-hold at street-corners, where tens of thousands of other foot passengers have
10 been slipping and sliding since the day broke (if this day ever broke), adding new deposits to the crust upon crust of mud, sticking at those points tenaciously to the pavement, and accumulating at compound interest.

Fog everywhere. Fog up the river, where it flows among green aits and meadows; fog down the river, where it rolls deified among the tiers of shipping and the waterside pollutions of a
15 great (and dirty) city. Fog on the Essex marshes, fog on the Kentish heights. Fog creeping into the cabooses of collier-brigs; fog lying out on the yards and hovering in the rigging of great ships; fog drooping on the gunwales of barges and small boats. Fog in the eyes and throats of ancient Greenwich pensioners, wheezing by the firesides of their wards; fog in the stem and bowl of the afternoon pipe of the wrathful skipper, down in his close cabin; fog cruelly
20 pinching the toes and fingers of his shivering little 'prentice boy on deck. Chance people on the bridges peeping over the parapets into a nether sky of fog, with fog all round them, as if they were up in a balloon and hanging in the misty clouds.

Gas looming through the fog in diverse places in the streets, much as the sun may, from the spongey fields, be seen to loom by husbandman and ploughboy. Most of the shops lighted two
25 hours before their time – as the gas seems to know, for it has a haggard and unwilling look.

The raw afternoon is rawest, and the dense fog is densest, and the muddy streets are muddiest near that leaden-headed old obstruction, appropriate ornament for the threshold of a leaden-headed old corporation, Temple Bar. And hard by Temple Bar, in Lincoln's Inn Hall, at the very
29 heart of the fog, sits the Lord High Chancellor in his High Court of Chancery.

Charles Dickens
(Extract)

After reading

Charles Dickens' description creates a powerful image of London smothered in mud and fog. The people and buildings are dirty, wet and cold, and everyday life is a struggle. Pedestrians slip over in the streets, while the Lord Chancellor in his court sits at the centre of the fog, as if the lawyers and the ancient courts are the source of the murky weather. It is a scene of stagnation and despair.

Activity 1

1. Dickens builds his description from a mix of concrete details, comparisons and comments. Refer back to the passage and record the line numbers where the following occur.

Details, comparisons and comments	Lines
a. A reference to the great flood mentioned in the Bible.	
b. A suggestion that the city looks primitive or prehistoric in the mud.	
c. An image of the dirty air.	
d. A reference to the fog invading people's bodies and personal spaces.	
e. Two descriptions of non-living things acting as if they were alive.	
f. A suggestion that the Chancellor and courts are contributing to the despair.	

2. Choose two of the above and discuss how each contributes to the effectiveness of the passage.

What's the use?

Description of this sort is often used to "set the scene" at the beginning of a story. When used in this way, the description has two purposes.

1. *Visualisation:* It helps the reader visualise the time and place.
2. *Theme:* It establishes a theme or *motif* that will run through the story.

In the extract from *Bleak House*, Dickens achieves both purposes. His description of the thick London fog not only gives a vivid sense of the physical environment but also introduces the theme of social stagnation. Like the thick fog, the legal system itself is choking the citizens in a haze of ancient rules and procedures.

In your own writing, this kind of description will be useful whenever you want to make a strong impression on your reader and provide *a vivid sense of time and place*. You might want to do these things in feature articles, letters, travel blogs and similar kinds of writing.

Good description is a source of pleasure to readers. In learning how to create rich and engaging descriptions, you will be learning a skill that contributes to your readers' enjoyment.

How much description?

The description in Dickens' passage is detailed and extended. A whole paragraph is devoted to the mud alone, and another to the fog. Not all descriptions are so detailed and elaborate. In deciding how much detail to include in a description, you should consider the *subject matter* and the *readership.* Subjects that are either unfamiliar or very significant demand more description. Similarly, work that will be read by the public will demand more care and attention than a piece written for yourself or someone you know.

Activity 2

1. Taking account of *subject matter* and *readership,* decide how much description you would use in the following cases. Rank the items from 1 (less detailed, fairly casual description) to 4 (very detailed, highly elaborate description).

    a. *Topic:* a letter describing a foreign city, where you are staying on holiday:

to a friend back home, who has also visited this city	☐
to a friend back home who has never visited this city	☐
in a blog for your personal website, to be read by family and friends	☐
in a blog for a commercial website run by a travel agency	☐

    b. *Topic:* a feature article about your town, written for a regional paper, describing:

everyday life	☐
an annual event, such as a fair or carnival	☐
a major calamity, such as a flood or fire	☐
your personal experiences growing up in the town	☐

    c. *Topic:* description of a place in:

a contemporary short story focussing mainly on character	☐
a chapter in a fantasy novel whose hero journeys to many different lands	☐
an introduction to a realistic novel about a single city and its people	☐
a parable or fable in which the location is unimportant	☐

2. Where else might you find detailed descriptions of time and place? List examples. (*Suggestions:* travel brochures? speeches marking major events? diaries? chronicles?)

Now that you have read the model and considered some possible uses of description, you are ready to learn about writing your own. Your goal will be to write a passage of description that imitates the style and structure of the piece by Dickens.

Step 2: Ideas and design

IN THIS SECTION:
- Learn to organise your ideas
- Learn to make a plan
- Write a first draft

Before you can learn to write an elaborate description like the extract from *Bleak House* by Charles Dickens you need to study how it has been constructed. We will start by looking at the ideas and the design of the passage.

Ideas: description and theme

The ideas developed in the passage are of two kinds.

1. *Description:* There are concrete descriptions of time and place.

2. *Theme:* There is a general theme that emerges from the overall picture.

The time and place is London in the winter of 1852. The theme is despair and stagnation. The *connection* between the concrete physical descriptions of time and place and the theme is an important element in the passage.

Description of place

When writing descriptions, good writers get most of their details from direct observation, not simply from imagination. Charles Dickens lived in London for much of his life and observed it closely. His knowledge of the city enabled him to choose real details for his description, even though his novel is fictional.

When writing about a place you know, you should spend some time carefully observing, and making notes on what you see. When writing about imaginary places, you should use your observation of real locations as a guide. Whether describing a city or a building, a face or a flower, you will need to consider all the features and properties that belong to the subject. From the range of features, you should then *select* those details that will create the impression you want to convey.

Elements of place: kinds of detail

In his description of London, Dickens has selected *three kinds of detail* that are effective in conveying the "character" of a place. You will use the same three categories in writing your own description.

1. *Physical features and landmarks:* Dickens refers to a number of London landmarks and to various locations by name: Lincoln's Inn, Holborn Hill, Essex. He also refers to characteristic physical features from the time period, such as chimney stacks and coal-ships. Place names, landforms and buildings are useful details to include.

2. *People and their activities:* People are a vital part of any description of place. In his description of London, Dickens describes pedestrians jostling one another, pensioners wheezing by their fires, and sailors on boats in the river. Classes, professions, activities and appearances are all useful details to include.

3. *The weather and climate:* Climate and weather make a place distinctive, and they have a powerful influence on a culture. A description of the weather can represent the mood and outlook of a people. In his description, Dickens emphasises the mud, the fog and the cold as a way of characterising the people's despair. References to day and night, seasons, the sky, and daily changes in weather can all be included.

Activity 3

1. Go back to the passage on page 3 and find examples of each of the following kinds of description. Highlight the examples, using different colours, labels or underlines for the three different categories.

   a. Descriptions of *physical features and landmarks*

   b. Descriptions of *people and their activities*

   c. Descriptions of *weather and climate*

2. What does your highlighting reveal about the *arrangement* of information in the passage?

   a. Are the three kinds of description kept separate, or are they woven together in the passage?

   b. Are the proportions of the kinds of description about equal, or is one kind given more attention than the others?

Choosing details

The key to creating effective description is *detail*. Readers need information to build their own picture of the scene being described. Well-chosen details will help make that picture seem complete and convincing.

When choosing details, you should consider three things: the *number and variety* of features to include, the *scale* of your details, and the *degree* of detail.

1. *Number and variety:* A rich description requires many supporting details. Dickens uses a large number of details to construct his picture of London in the winter. These include: mud on street corners; smoke falling from chimneys; mud-spattered dogs and horses; pedestrians with umbrellas; and so on. The variety of details covers all of the elements in roughly equal proportion: physical features, people and activities, and weather.

2. *Scale:* Dickens uses large-scale and small-scale details to create his description. Large-scale details help build the "big picture" of London. They include references to streets, localities, rivers, bridges, and buildings. Small-scale details help develop a more personal or intimate picture, like a camera close-up. They include the smoke and fog in the boat captain's pipe, and the cold air pinching the fingers and toes of the apprentice. The combination of "big" and "small" details makes the description seem rich and complete.

3. *Degree:* The degree of detail in a description can range from general to specific to specific *and* detailed. Compare these descriptions.

    General: The roadways were lined with mud.
    Specific: Fleet Street was lined with mud.
    Detailed: Fleet Street was lined with brown mud, like a silted river.

    General: Travellers peered into the fog.
    Specific: The crew on the morning ferry peered into the fog.
    Detailed: The ferry pilot in his cramped wheelhouse peered into the murky fog.

Detailed, specific descriptions give the reader more information with which to form an impression of the scene. They also make a description more convincing, by creating the impression of first-hand knowledge. Dickens often describes specific examples rather than broad classes of things. In his description, the details convince us that he knows London and has actually seen these things. Without such details, the feeling of authenticity might be lost.

Activity 4

1. Dickens' description of London is built up from many details. Re-read the passage and find four more details to add to this list.

   a. mud on street corners   e. ....

   b. smoke falling from chimneys   f. ....

   c. mud-spattered dogs and horses   g. ....

   d. pedestrians with umbrellas   h. ....

2. How many features of London are actually included in the description by Dickens? Make a count of the *total number of things* described in the passage.

3. Decide whether the following are large-scale or small-scale details. Tick the appropriate box for each of the details listed below.

Details	Large	Small
a. Lincoln's Inn Hall		
b. mud in the streets		
c. flakes of soot in the smoke		
d. mud on street-corner pavements		
e. fog up-river and down-river		
f. fog on the Essex marshes and the Kentish heights		
g. fog in the throats of pensioners		
h. fog freezing fingers and toes		

4. Invent *four* more details that could be added to the passage. Make two of them large-scale details, and two small-scale details. Viewing some images of "old" London might help you.

   (*Some suggestions:* Big Ben; the palace guards; chimney sweeps; the East End; flower sellers; shop windows; a policeman's whistle; a horse and carriage; a coal cellar; gentlemen in top hats.)

> **Descriptions: four rules**
>
> 1. To convey the "character" of a place, references are made to physical features and landmarks; people and their activities; the weather and climate.
>
> 2. A large number and variety of details are included in the description.
>
> 3. Large-scale details (e.g. rivers, bridges, buildings) help build the "big picture"; small-scale details help develop a more intimate picture like a camera close-up (e.g. leaves on a wet pavement).
>
> 4. The degree of detail can range from general to specific and detailed. Specific *and* detailed descriptions give the reader more information with which to form an impression of the scene.

Theme

Through his description, Dickens develops a theme of despair and stagnation. The people of London seem trapped by the weather, shut off from one another and the world. The mud and fog saturate both the physical environment and the social institutions.

Dickens develops the theme by *selecting* and *repeating* certain details of his description. He emphasises the mud and the fog, linking them to every aspect of the city: the streets, the buildings, the people, and even the legal system. The result is an overwhelming impression of the city being saturated by the fog, to the point of immobility.

> **Developing a theme: two rules**
>
> 1. *Select* descriptive details that match and reinforce the impression you want to create.
>
> 2. *Emphasise* the details through repetition.

Activity 5

1. On the next page is a chart showing examples of *descriptions* of places. Read the *descriptions* in column A, and match each to a suitable *theme* chosen from the list above the chart. Write your choice of theme in column B. Then choose a *detail* from the description that you would emphasise to help build that theme. Write your choice of detail in column C.

   To help you, the first row on the chart uses the passage from *Bleak House* as an example. In column A there is a *description of place*; in column B there is a "matching" *theme*; and in column C there is a *detail* that might be emphasised through repetition to build the theme.

Themes: a. the past, gloomy pessimism; b. technology and power; c. nature, harmony, health; d. energy, optimism, the future; e. corruption, danger, criminality; f. sickness, disease, decline of civilisation; g. life's long journey, the progress of mankind

A. Description of place	B. Theme	C. Emphasis
London. A city mired in mud and fog; pedestrians slipping and jostling in the streets; ships and bridges obscured; the courthouse and chancellor surrounded by fog.	*Stagnation, a society "trapped" and static.*	*The fog.*
1. A remote country town. Houses with broken front fences; wrecked cars dotted beside the main roads; clouds in the sky and a cold wind; a hotel with silent drinkers at the bar, women playing slot machines.		
2. A town built on swampland. Damp and rotting buildings; misty air; abandoned, unfinished buildings; mosquitoes; workers lazing idly; elderly pedestrians wheezing.		
3. A road at the edge of a jungle. Heat and humidity; a car at a checkpoint guarded by soldiers with guns; animal sounds; logging trucks on the road; the sound of a shotgun; a military commander in his office.		
4. A tropical island. Palm trees, clean beaches, blue sky; a gleaming five-star hotel and a boat marina; tourists at street markets; local children playing on the beach; the sound of the ocean.		
5. A city. Freeways and cars, electric railways and escalators, buses and ferries; busy people in sharp suits, with brief-cases and mobile phones; impressive office buildings lit up brightly at night.		
6. A floating village of boats on a long and winding river. Fishermen unloading their catches; vendors selling noodles and fish at markets on the jetties; container ships loaded with luxury cars.		
7. A modern city. Skyscrapers of steel and glass; heat and sunshine, blue sky; office workers and shoppers bustling; cars, noise and glare; cranes on buildings; dealers shouting in the stock exchange.		

2. Look again at description 7 in the chart. Imagine you are writing a description of a modern city. Your *theme* is *optimism, energy and the future.* Your *emphasis* is *heat and sunshine.*

    Here are twelve additional details that could be included in a description of the city. Choose *six* that you think are most appropriate to the topic and theme. Tick your choices.

    a. toffee wrappers trodden into cracks in the pavement ☐
    b. plastic rubbish bags floating in the harbour ☐
    c. fountains in the marble lobbies of office buildings ☐
    d. yellow cranes crouched high over rising towers ☐
    e. gold rings on the manicured fingers of executives ☐
    f. studded Gucci handbags glinting in Smith Street shop windows ☐
    g. a busker with his accordion and his monkey, collecting tips ☐
    h. shining chrome tables and chairs at the cafes in Collins Square ☐
    i. a white speedboat on the water ☐
    j. construction workers in hard hats and sunglasses ☐
    k. the chime of a mobile phone echoing in the mall ☐
    l. red silk ties on blue-suited businessmen ☐

3. Based on your experience or observation of large modern cities add *four* more details that emphasise heat, sunshine and activity. Make sure you include an item from each of the categories: physical features and landmarks; people and their activities; weather and climate.

    ....

    ....

    ....

    ....

4. Refer back to your four new features, above, and consider the selections you have made.

    a. Have you used *large-scale* and *small-scale* details?
    b. Have you used different *degrees of detail?*

5. Compare your details with those of others in your group or class. Build a combined list of about 20 of the best details, with a mix of scale and degree. Save these for later.

Design: the frame

The complex ideas in Dickens' description of London have been carefully arranged to make the image seem whole and complete. This has been done using a *literary frame*.

Just as a picture frame makes a painting seem finished and complete, a literary frame creates a pleasing sense of order and completeness for the description. In Dickens' description of London, the frame is made up of a brief *introduction* and a closing *summary*. These "contain" or frame the elaboration of details and impressions. Some elements of the introduction are repeated in the summary.

Introduction: *Statement of time and place plus first details.*
London. November weather. The Lord Chancellor in Lincoln's Inn.

Description: *Details and impressions reinforce description and build theme.*

Mud in the streets
"As much mud in the streets as if the waters had but newly retired from the from the face of the earth..."

Smoke in the air
"Smoke lowering down from chimney-pots, making a soft, black drizzle, with flakes of soot in it..."

Animals and people
"Dogs, undistinguishable in the mire. Horses, scarcely better... Foot passengers, jostling one another's umbrellas..."

Fog
"Fog everywhere. Fog up the river... fog down the river... on the Essex marshes... on the Kentish heights... in the rigging of great ships... in the eyes and throats... pinching the toes and fingers..."

Gas
"Gas looming through the fog in diverse places in the streets... it has a haggard and unwilling look."

Frame

Summary: *Restates key ideas and repeats first detail.*
Mud and fog; the Lord Chancellor at the centre of the fog.

Activity 6

1. Go back to the passage by Charles Dickens on page 3 and mark out where exactly you think these framing sections begin and end. Then label the passage to show the three sections.

2. Dickens' description has a clear design with a number of identifiable features. Complete the chart below with examples from the passage from *Bleak House*.

Features of the description	Examples
It uses a frame to organise the description. (Name the sections, and the number of lines in each.)	
It uses direct statement to introduce the time and place. (Name the city and the time.)	
It names specific physical features and landmarks. (List three examples.)	
It emphasises aspects of the weather. (Name the aspect of weather emphasised.)	
It uses large-scale and small-scale details. (Give examples.)	
It develops a theme. (State the theme.)	
It uses an *anachronism* (a reference to an earlier time). (Name the reference.)	

Another example

Framing your descriptions is an excellent technique to learn. It is a strategy used often by Dickens, and also by many modern writers.

The contemporary novelist, Robert Harris, has used the same design for the opening of his novel *Enigma,* which was published in 1995. The story is a thriller set in England during the Second World War. It tells of secret code-breaking operations that helped the Allies read German military signals.

In the following short extract from the novel, the English town of Cambridge is described as a timeless "ghost town" that is returned to the "Middle Ages" by the blackout and the war. The extract shows that the principles of good description can be used even in very short passages.

Activity 7

1. Read the extract below closely, looking for any similarities to the description from *Bleak House*.

Enigma
Cambridge in the fourth winter of the war: a ghost town.

A ceaseless Siberian wind with nothing to blunt its edge for eight thousand miles whipped up off the North Sea and swept low across the Fens. It rattled the signs to the air-raid shelters in Trinity New Court and battered on the boarded up windows of King's College Chapel. It prowled through the quadrangles and staircases, confining the few dons and students still in residence to their rooms. By mid-afternoon, the narrow cobbled streets were deserted. By nightfall, with not a light to be seen, the university was returned to a darkness it hadn't known since the Middle Ages. A procession of monks shuffling over Magdalene Bridge on their way to Vespers would scarcely have seemed out of place.

In the wartime blackout, the centuries had dissolved.

2. Although it is brief, Harris's description has a lot in common with Dickens'. You can see this clearly by completing the same chart as you did to analyse the features of the description in the extract from *Bleak House*. Go back to the chart on page 14 and complete it with examples of the descriptive features from the passage from *Enigma*.

> Literary framing of a description: three rules
> 1. Begin with a statement of time and place, giving initial details of the scene.
> 2. Add to and develop the details and impressions, which reinforce the description and build a theme.
> 3. End with a brief summary that restates the initial details.

Planning your own description

Now that you have studied the ideas and the design of Dickens' description, and compared it with another example, you can begin to plan your own. For your first attempt, you will describe a modern city, based on the topic and starting points given in Activity 5 on page 10.

Activity 8

Use the chart on the next page to plan your first draft of a description of a modern city called Metropolis. Complete the blank sections of the plan by listing in *note form* only the details you will add. Some suggestions and starting points have been included for you. You can also use ideas from Activity 5 (number 2) on page 12.

Plan for a description of a place

Ideas

Place:	A modern city, "Metropolis"
Theme:	Optimism, energy, the future
Emphasis:	Heat and sunshine

Details:	List about 20 details that describe: a. the physical place (features and landmarks) b. the people and their activities c. the climate of heat and sunshine (e.g. construction workers sweating in hard hats and sunglasses...)

Design

Introduction: *State time and place plus first details*

a. State the place and the time with a detail to set the scene.
   (e.g. "Metropolis. The holiday season over. Dealers shouting in the stock exchange.")

   ....

b. What other details will you mention? List them.

   ....

Description: *Add details and impressions to reinforce description and build theme*

a. List the details you will include to develop the impression of heat and activity.
   (e.g. "As much heat in the air as if the sun itself had burst...")

   ....

b. List details you will include to emphasise the impression of sunlight.
   (e.g. "Sun everywhere. Sun on the...")

   ....

Remember: Include physical features, people, weather. Include large- and small-scale items.

Summary: *Restate key ideas and repeat a first detail*

List the details you will repeat from your description.
(e.g. "The afternoon is hottest and the sunlight brightest...")

....

Activity 9

Once you have made your plan, go on and write the first draft of your description. Do your best to imitate the design and writing style of the description by Charles Dickens on page 3. Do not worry if your first draft is not yet very polished.

> When you have written your draft, put it to one side. You will return to it as you work through the following section on style.

Copying or dictation

Study closely the first six lines of the opening paragraph of Dickens' description on page 3. Pay attention to these things:

1. The length and wording of the sentences

2. The punctuation used

3. The spelling (especially the spelling of unfamiliar words)

Copy the lines into your notebook, checking against the original as you go. Make sure you capture the wording and punctuation exactly. Alternatively, write out the lines as your teacher reads them aloud. When you are done, discuss any features of the writing that have come to your attention.

Step 3: Style

IN THIS SECTION:
- Learn the writer's techniques
- Study diction, sentence patterns, and special features
- Improve your draft in stages

Now that you have studied the overall design of Dickens' description, it is time to examine the style – that is, the way words, sentences and other techniques are used in the writing. The description of London has a very definite style, which you will imitate in your writing. The activities that follow will help you learn about three main features of the style: *diction, sentence patterns,* and *techniques of description.*

Diction

The term *diction* refers to the words that are used in the writing. The choice and arrangement of words has a powerful effect on the reader, and is one of your main tools for shaping the tone and style of your description.

Compare these two sentences.

> *Sentence A:* As much mud in the streets as if the waters had but newly retired from the face of the earth, and it would not be wonderful to meet a Megalosaurus, forty feet long or so, waddling like an elephantine lizard up Holborn Hill.

> *Sentence B:* As much mud in the streets as if the Flood had just ended, and it wouldn't be a surprise to see a dinosaur forty feet long waddling like a giant lizard up Holborn Hill.

These sentences say much the same thing, but their "feel" is quite different. Sentence A is more wordy than B, and seems dense and complex to read. It matches the dense and complex description of the physical conditions in London. Sentence B seems "lighter" and easier to read. The difference is partly a product of word-choice, or diction.

While some sentences in Dickens' description seem dense and complex, others are simpler and much more direct. For example:

> Fog everywhere... fog all round them, as if they were up in a balloon and hanging in the misty clouds.

With such variations in the diction, it can be difficult to identify the consistent features of the language. Doing so requires a close analysis of the passage.

Activity 10

1. Decide which of the following statements about sentences A and B on the previous page, are true or false. Place a tick in the apropriate column below.

Sentence	True	False
a. A contains more long words than B.		
b. A is more abstract than B.		
c. A uses more old-fashioned words than B.		
d. A is less direct than B.		
e. A uses more adjectives than B.		
f. A has a more complex word order than B.		

2. You can analyse the diction in any piece of writing by counting how often certain features appear. Use the following table to identify and count some features of the language in the extract from *Bleak House* on page 3. Write your results in the right-hand column. (A more complete table can be found on page 148.)

Features	Number
Number of concrete nouns (e.g. stone, rain, bread, mud)	
Number of abstract nouns (e.g. beauty, love, honesty, loneliness)	
Number of single syllable words (e.g. eat, work, food)	
Number of multi-syllable words (e.g. consume, labour, nourishment)	
Number of active verbs (e.g. Rain swamping the pavement)	
Number of passive verbs (e.g. The pavement is swamped by rain.)	
Number of adjectives (e.g. red rose, fair hair, honest gentleman, biggest fish)	

3. After doing the analysis, have any of your answers to question 1. above changed?

You may have been surprised, for example, to find that the diction in Dickens description consists mostly of concrete nouns and active verbs. There are relatively few adjectives.

Dickens' diction

Your study of the extract from *Bleak House* should have revealed the main features of the diction, some of which are quite surprising.

1. *Concrete nouns:* The writing is filled with familiar concrete nouns, such as "mud", "fog", "smoke", "soot", "dogs", "horses", and "street-corners". There are relatively few abstract ideas, such as "mourning". Dickens uses occasional large words, such as "elephantine" and "tenaciously" – but they are not as common as the simpler, single-syllable words that make up most of the passage.

2. *Active verbs:* The use of verbs in the writing is also interesting. Most verbs are in the active form, but they describe sluggish actions that involve very little movement: "lowering", "creeping", "lying", "drooping", "pinching", "looming", "wheezing". These verbs help to create a sense of stillness and stagnation.

3. *Few adjectives:* Perhaps the biggest surprise is that the passage contains few adjectives. Beginning writers often cram too many adjectives into their descriptions, believing that adjectives add detail. Dickens, however, creates detail through the sheer number of items he includes in his description, and through his control of scale and degree.

The impression of wordiness in some sections of the description is mainly a result of two properties: the use of *some* multisyllable words (e.g. "elephantine" instead of "giant") and the use of *some* long phrases ("retired from the face of the earth", instead of "receded").

In your own descriptions, you should follow the example of using concrete nouns, active verbs and few adjectives. But you should adjust the length of words and phrases to suit your topic. To create a sense of energy and movement, use shorter words and phrases.

Diction: three rules
1. Use simple concrete nouns.

2. Use active verbs.

3. Use few adjectives.

Activity 11

1. Rewrite the following sentences so that they contain simple concrete nouns. (*Hint:* change the underlined words.)

    Example: <u>Members of the business professions</u> bustling in their <u>places of employment.</u>
    Re-written: Businessmen bustling in their offices.

    a. <u>White-hulled motorised watercraft</u> jetting through the harbour.
    b. <u>Employees in formal clothing</u> chatting over coffee.
    c. <u>Office infrastructure</u> casting sharp shadows on the <u>transport routes</u>.

2. Choose the best verb to help create a sense of energy and action in these sentences.

    a. Sunshine (bouncing, glancing, reflecting) off glass-walled buildings.
    b. Brokers at the stock exchange (shouting, baying, calling) to buy.
    c. Cranes (crouching, resting, sitting) on high sunlit towers.

3. The following sentences contain many adjectives (words describing colour, shape, and size). Reduce the number of adjectives to make the details stand out.

    a. Bright, energetic, young women in suits striding to work, holding coffee in large, white-lidded paper cups.
    b. Stocky construction workers in blue shirts and yellow plastic hard-hats, a film of glistening perspiration on their foreheads.
    c. The bright, yellow sun, a glowing rivet in the pale, blue, cloudless sky.

Go back to your draft description of the city of Metropolis, and review the diction. Check that you are using concrete nouns and active verbs to build the theme of optimism and energy. Keep the number of adjectives to a minimum.

Sentence patterns

Sentence patterns play a vital role in Dickens' description of London. Three important sentence properties are:

1. length and variety
2. use of sentence fragments, compounds and lists
3. use of repetition.

Activity 12

1. Do a counting analysis of the following sentence features in the extract on page 3. Record your findings in the first column on the right under "Dickens".

Sentences	Dickens	Draft
Total number of sentences		
Length of longest sentence		
Length of shortest sentence		
Average sentence length		
Number of sentence fragments (subject without a verb, e.g. People everywhere. Rain falling.)		
Number of simple sentences (one main clause, e.g. The tall man pushed in.)		
Number of compounds (two or more clauses, e.g. The tall man pushed in; the others waited.)		
Number of complex sentences (main clause with subordinate clauses, e.g. The tall man pushed through, hardly slowing down.)		

Your analysis should have shown that there is great variety in the length and type of sentences used in the description by Dickens. The shortest sentence is only one word in length, while the longest is over 60 words, with many different lengths in between.

2. Use the table now to analyse your draft description. Record your findings in the second column. How closely does your description match Dickens' description in its:

    a. length of sentences?
    b. use of sentence fragments?
    c. other sentence patterns?

Fragments

One of the most striking features in Dickens' passage is the use of sentence *fragments*. These are sentences that have no main verb.

Compare these examples.

Sentence	Fragment
Michaelmas term was lately over.	Michaelmas term lately over.
The November weather was implacable.	Implacable November weather.
Dogs were undistinguishable in mire.	Dogs, undistinguishable in mire.
The fog was everywhere.	Fog everywhere.

Sentence fragments make the passage feel like a list of notes or jottings. The details seem heaped up from direct observation. This is a trick Dickens learned as a newspaper reporter. It creates an eye-witness impression.

Compounds

A second interesting feature is the use of sentence *compounds*. Dickens often links short sentences together using a comma or semi-colon. This technique reinforces the impression of listing. For example:

"Fog up the river, where it flows...; fog down the river, where it rolls..."

"Fog on the Essex marshes; fog on the Kentish heights."

"Fog creeping into the cabooses...; fog lying out on the yards...; fog drooping on the gunwales..."

"Fog in the eyes and throats...; fog in the stem and bowl..."

In these examples, the sentences are written in *parallel form,* which means the order of words is repeated in each part of the sentence.

Repetitions – anaphora

Dickens also begins many sentences with the same word, especially in the second paragraph of the passage on page 3. The word "fog" is used at the beginning of ten sentences or clauses in a row. This technique of *repeating* a word at the start of each sentence is called *anaphora*. It draws attention to the repeated idea, and creates the impression that it cannot be escaped.

> Sentences: four rules
>
> 1. Sentence fragments are used to create an observational style.
>
> 2. Short sentences are linked, using commas or semi-colons, to create compounds that pile detail upon detail.
>
> 3. A key word is repeated at the front of sentences, to emphasise an idea and make it seem inescapable.
>
> 4. Sentence lengths are varied: short sentences to suggest energy; long sentences to slow the pace.

Activity 13

1. Convert these sentences into fragments, to create short notes. (*Hint:* remove unnecessary verbs, such as "was" and "were".)

   a. Mobile phones were chiming in the mall.
   b. The sun was shining on studded Gucci handbags in shop windows.
   c. Workers on lunchbreak were laughing in the arcades.
   d. Pigeons were stealing crumbs from under cafe tables.

2. Punctuate this paragraph using commas and semi-colons to create a *single* compound sentence.

   Heat seeping into the shade beneath trees. Heat shimmering on the rooflines of office buildings. Heat wavering on the pavement of the shopping mall. Heat rolling over the river, where it breathes on the manicured lawns of the mansions and on the gleaming windows of utilities parked in curving driveways.

3. Rewrite this paragraph so that all of the sentences, and main clauses within sentences, begin with the same word: *Sun.*

   Sun on the downtown plazas and on the uptown parks. There was sun reflected like a glowing rivet in the dark glasses of construction workers. More sun bouncing off chrome chairs and tables in the sidewalk cafes. Between the oily waves in the boat harbour, the sun was wobbling like a poaching egg.

> Go back to your draft description and check the number, length and type of sentences. Do you have as much variety as Dickens? If not, look for ways to vary the length of your sentences. Check that you have used sentence fragments and compounds to create an impression of listing, and repetition to emphasise the sunshine.

Special features: comparison, personification, anachronism

In addition to recording details of the scene, Dickens uses a variety of techniques to make his descriptions more powerful or effective. These techniques intensify the description by drawing creative connections between things.

Comparison

The most direct technique for intensifying a description is to make a comparison. Comparing one thing to another is an efficient way of conveying ideas without having to spell them out. The following are some comparisons that can be found in the passage.

muddy streets	*compared to*	the aftermath of the Flood
people on a bridge	*compared to*	passengers in a hot-air balloon
flakes of soot	*compared to*	snowflakes in mourning

Comparisons like these can work in a number of ways. They may help describe the scene by referring to something already familiar to the reader; or they may draw attention to the scene by referring to something unfamiliar. There are two important rules for making effective comparisons: the things compared must share some physical properties, and share similar associations or meanings. For example, flakes of soot and snowflakes are physically similar in size and behaviour (both fall gently out of the air); but a snowflake is white and clean, while soot is black. By describing the soot as black snowflakes "in mourning", Dickens introduces ideas of death and decay that give similar meanings to the two things.

Personification

Inanimate objects and elements, like buildings or fog, become more interesting when described as if they were capable of thinking and acting – that is, as if they were living things. This technique is often called personification, but its technical name is *prosopopoeia*. (*Prosopon* is Greek for "face", and the word *prosopopoeia* literally means "making a face".) The following are examples of objects that are "given a face" – or made into living things – in Dickens' description. The objects are described in terms of actions they perform.

Object	*Action*
The smoke and soot	gone into mourning
The fog	creeps into cabooses, droops on boats, pinches toes
The gas	looks haggard and unwilling

These are subtle descriptions. Dickens does not say, "The fog reached out its ghostly arm and pinched the apprentice's toes." Instead, he applies verbs ("pinch") or adjectives ("unwilling"), which we associate with people, *directly* to the objects he is describing.

Anachronism

Charles Dickens makes his dreary London seem primitive by inserting a description from prehistoric times: the image of a megalosaurus waddling up a hill. In the same way, Robert Harris makes his ghostly Cambridge seem like a town from the "Middle Ages", by imagining medieval monks walking to their prayers. These are both *anachronisms,* which means details "misplaced in time".

As with comparisons, an anachronism must be *physically appropriate* to the place being described. It must convey *associations* that match the scene. A megalosaurus seems suited to the dank and muddy scene of London in 1852, but a primitive beach-dwelling crab or a grasshopper would not be.

Inserting an anachronism into a description is a useful way of signalling that a place is either old-fashioned or futuristic.

Activity 14

1. Based on physical properties and associations, which of the following are suitable to describe a modern, energetic, fast-growing city? Give reasons for your choices.

    a. The sun compared to a glowing rivet, shining on construction workers. ☐

    b. Cranes compared to praying mantises crouched on tall buildings. ☐

    c. Freeways compared to arteries carrying the city's life blood. ☐

    d. Steel and glass skyscrapers compared to crystals growing skyward on invisible strings. ☐

2. Rewrite these personifications so that they are more subtle. (*Hint:* use a single verb to suggest human action, rather than a long description with lots of adjectives and adverbs.)

    a. The heat lolling its lazy, invisible body in parks and walkways.

    ....

    b. Mischievous fingers of sunlight tickling the carp in city ponds.

    ....

    c. Hotel lobbies breathing cool air into the hazy streets, like great frost giants.

    ....

    d. Street lights blinking their neon eyes impassively at impatient pedestrians.

    ....

3. Which two of the following *anachronisms* are best for describing a futuristic modern city? Give reasons for your choices.

"So much technology and luxury, it would not be surprising to see...

   a. a space-port in the central square, where sleek rockets whisk travellers into the sky."

   b. blank-faced robots calmly pumping petrol at the service stations."

   c. computers with mechanical arms serving coffee at sidewalk cafes."

   d. patient android servants staffing the counters in expensive department stores."

Go back to your draft description of Metropolis and consider whether you could use comparisons, personifications or anachronisms to intensify your description. Add at least one of these techniques to your writing.

You have now finished revising your draft description.

Go to Step 4 on page 28 if you want more practice in diction, sentence patterns and descriptive figures.

OR

Go straight to Step 5 on page 30 to write your final copy.

Step 4: Exercises (optional)

IN THIS SECTION:
■ Practise your new skills

Do you need more practice in the new writing skills you have learned? The exercises that follow will give you more preparation in diction and sentence styles. Answers are on page 36. When you feel confident in the skills, go on to Step 5 on page 30 and write the final copy of your description.

1. *Diction – verbs:* Choose the best verb to help create a sense of energy and action in these sentences.

    a. Cars (rolling, darting, advancing) through narrow streets.

    b. Wind (gusting, curling, whipping) around corners.

    c. Shadows (sliding, creeping, stretching) out from buildings.

    d. Walkers (strutting, scuttling, ambling) through shopping malls.

2. *Diction – adjectives:* Reduce the number of adjectives to make the key details stand out.

    a. Cool, clear water bubbling in hard, shiny, marble fountains.

    b. Sun playing on the colourful, shining gems in jewellers' windows.

    c. Traffic rumbling like low, dull thunder through the long, straight canyons of glass.

    d. The pale, blue sky stretched thin over the vast, angular, steel skyline.

3. *Sentences – fragments:* Convert these sentences into fragments, to create short notes.

    a. The sun was climbing slowly into the morning sky.

    b. The wind was blowing irresistibly through the narrow alleys.

    c. The small waves were lapping at the harbour wall.

    d. Diverse people were lunching in the park.

4. *Sentences – repetition:* Rewrite the paragraph below so that all of the sentences, and main clauses within sentences, begin with the same word – *wind*. Use semi-colons to arrange the sentences into compounds.

    Wind blowing high among flag poles and aerials, and blowing low among waste bins and hydrants. The wind scattering leaves in the parks. The spray of sprinklers driven onto roads and passing cars by the wind. Wind flicking the coats and collars of pedestrians, who clasp their arms in front and push against the gales.

5. *Descriptive figures – personifications:* Rewrite these personifications so that they are more subtle.

    a. The warm sun turned its round, yellow face and smiled gently on the children's cheeks.

    b. The smoke curled its thin arms comfortingly around the ageing chimney.

    c. Two large windows silently stared like glassy eyes across the harbour.

6. *Descriptive figures – anachronisms:* Write short anachronisms using the following details. Use the pattern: "So much... it would not be surprising..."

    An example is shown below.

    Details: A city of steel and glass. Sunlight reflecting off buildings.

    Anachronism: *So much* light bouncing off glass buildings *it would not be surprising* to discover shining spaceships shooting death rays down the boulevard.

    a. A modern pine forest. A sauropod munching on ferns.

    b. A country town. Bushrangers riding through the street.

    c. A historic building. Knights in armour on chargers.

Step 5: The final copy

IN THIS SECTION:
- Put it all together
- Write the final copy
- Hand it in

Now you are ready to write the final version of your description. Try to imitate closely the design and style of the passage by Dickens.

On page 31 is a checklist you or your teacher can use to assess your work.

Summary: Formula for describing a place

Purpose
To create a powerful impression of time and place; to set the scene for a story.

Ideas
- Include descriptions of physical features and landmarks; people and actions; climate and weather.
- Develop an overriding theme for your description.
- Use details to build your description that are:
  - many and varied
  - small-scale and large-scale
  - specific and general

Design
- Use a framing arrangement, consisting of:
  - a direct statement of time and place, with initial details
  - details and impressions that reinforce the description and build a theme
  - a brief summary that restates an initial detail, to end the description

Style
- *Diction:* use concrete nouns, active verbs and few adjectives.
- *Sentences:* consider sentence fragments, compounds, lists and repetitions.
- *Figures:* consider using comparisons, personification, and anachronisms.

Assessment checklist: Project 1

Score your work as follows: 2 points for each *Yes;* 1 point for *Partly;* 0 points for each *No.* Add the scores for a mark out of 20.

Project 1: Write a description of place	
Ideas	**Tick the box**
Does the description offer the reader a powerful impression of a place?	No ☐ Partly ☐ Yes ☐
Are there detailed descriptions of physical features, people and activities, and weather and climate?	No ☐ Partly ☐ Yes ☐
Is there a clear theme to the description, reinforced through repetition?	No ☐ Partly ☐ Yes ☐
Design	
Has a frame been used to arrange the material? Is it effective?	No ☐ Partly ☐ Yes ☐
Are the details of the scene well-balanced? (In number and variety, in scale, and in degree?)	No ☐ Partly ☐ Yes ☐
Style	
Is the diction correct? (Does it feature concrete nouns, active verbs, and few adjectives?)	No ☐ Partly ☐ Yes ☐
Are the sentences correctly formed? (Consider length and variety, use of fragments and compounds, and use of repetition.)	No ☐ Partly ☐ Yes ☐
Are descriptive figures used correctly? (Consider comparison, personification, anachronism.)	No ☐ Partly ☐ Yes ☐
Spelling and punctuation	
Are all of the words spelled correctly?	No ☐ Partly ☐ Yes ☐
Is the punctuation correct, especially the punctuation of compounds?	No ☐ Partly ☐ Yes ☐
Comment:	
Date:	Score:

Going further

IN THIS SECTION:
■ Get ideas for further writing

1. Write an original description of a real place you know well. Here are four possible topics.

   Suggestions:

   a. Your school, college, university or workplace
   b. Your home town, street, or suburb
   c. A city you know well
   d. A rural area

   Follow the steps from the plan on page 16:

   a. Choose your topic.
   b. Observe the scene, and record details in a notepad.
   c. Decide on a theme that matches the location.
   d. Select some details to emphasise.

   Experiment with the techniques you have learned, such as: using sentence fragments and compounds; using comparisons, personification and anachronisms.

2. Describe an *imaginary* place, using the techniques you have learned on this project.

   Suggestions:

   a. A fantasy or science fiction setting from a film.
   b. A setting based on a computer game you have played.
   c. A location of your own invention.
   d. Any of the topics from Activity 5 on page 11.

3. Collect five detailed descriptions of places, from a range of written sources. Search in novels, travel brochures, travel blogs, news magazines, and the like. Analyse some features of the design and writing style, using the recording sheets on pages 148–151.

   Use the information to do one of the following:

   a. Prepare a report on your findings about the techniques of description used.
   b. Write a description using the design and style of one of the pieces you have found.

Quiz: Project 1

1. Give a definition of "description", and say where the word comes from.

   ....

2. Descriptions of place are often used to set the scene in novels and stories. State two purposes for such a description.

   ....

3. State three facts about the author Charles Dickens.

   ....

4. Give the date of publication for *Bleak House*, and name two other works by Dickens.

   ....

5. Name three elements that should be included in a description of place.

   ....

6. Explain the concept of *scale* in a description and give two examples.

   ....

7. State three rules for *diction* in a description of place.

   ....

8. Name three features of the sentences used in Dickens' description.

   ....

9. State three techniques for intensifying a description.

   ....

10. Explain the following: *anaphora, prosopopoeia, anachronism.*

   ....

Answers for Project 1 Activities

These are suggested answers. In some cases your wording may differ slightly. If in doubt, check with your teacher.

Activity	Page	Answers
1	4	a. Lines 2–3; b. Lines 3–4; c. Lines 5–6; d. Lines 17–22; e. Smoke: Lines 5–6; Fog: Lines 15–17; 19–20; Gas: Line 25; f. Lines 27–29.
	5	1. *Level 1* (less detailed) topics: From Section a. A letter to a friend back home, who has also visited this city; Section b. Describing everyday life; Section c. In a parable or fable in which the location is unimportant. *Level 4* (very detailed) topics: From Section a. A blog for a commercial website run by a travel agency; Section b. Describing a major calamity, such as a flood or fire; Section c. For the introduction to a realistic novel about a single city and its people. *Intermediate levels:* discuss with your teacher. 2. Check with your teacher.
3	7	1. Check with your teacher. 2. a. and b. The elements are woven together in roughly equal proportion.
4	9	1. This is a self-checking activity. 2. There are about 20 separate details in the passage. 3. Large-scale items are a, b, e, f; small-scale items are: c, d, g and h. 4. Check with your teacher.
5	10–12	1. Suggested pairs: 1a, 2f, 3e, 4c, 5b, 6g, 7d. Possible emphases: check with your teacher. 2. Suitable choices would be any of these: c, d, e, f, h, i, j, k, l. 3. 4 and 5. Check with your teacher.
6	14	1. and 2. Check with your teacher.
7	15	1. and 2. Check with your teacher.
8	15	Check with your teacher.
9	17	This is a self-checking task.
10	19	1. a.T; b.F; c.T; d.F; e.F; f.F. 2. and 3. Check with your teacher.

11	21	1. a. speedboats, b. workers, suits, c. buildings, roads (any similar answers will do).
		 2. a. bouncing, b. baying, c. crouching (these suggest the strongest actions).
		 3. a. Young women in suits striding to work, holding coffee in paper cups.
		     b. Construction workers in hard hats, perspiration on their foreheads.
		     c. The sun a glowing rivet in the sky. (This is a matter of judgement. Some adjectives could be retained.)

12	22	1. Check with your teacher. 2. This is a self-checking task.

Activity	Page	Answers

13	24	1. a. Mobile phones chiming in the mall.
		   b. Sun shining on studded Gucci handbags in shop windows.
		   c. Workers on lunchbreak laughing in the arcades.
		   d. Pigeons stealing crumbs from under cafe tables.
		2. Heat seeping into the shade beneath trees; heat shimmering on the rooflines of office buildings; heat wavering on the pavement of the shopping mall; heat rolling over the river, where it breathes on the manicured lawns of the mansions and on the gleaming windows of utilities parked in curving driveways.
		3. Sun on the downtown plazas; sun on the uptown parks. Sun reflected like a glowing rivet in the dark glasses of construction workers. Sun bouncing off chrome chairs and tables in the sidewalk cafes. Sun wobbling like a poaching egg between the oily waves in the boat harbour.

14	26–27	1. Better choices are a. and d. (Other choices could be argued for.)
		2. a. Heat lolling in parks and walkways.
		   b. Sunlight tickling the carp in city ponds.
		   c. Hotel lobbies breathing cool air into the hazy streets.
		   d. Street lights blinking impassively at impatient pedestrians.
		3. Best choices are a. or d.

Answers for Project 1 Exercises

These are suggested answers. In some cases your wording may differ slightly. If in doubt, check with your teacher.

Exercise title	Page	Answers
1. Diction – verbs:	28	a. darting; b. whipping; c. stretching; d. scuttling.
2. Diction – adjectives:	28	a. Clear water bubbling in marble fountains. b. Sun playing on gems in jewellers' windows. c. Traffic rumbling like thunder through canyons of glass. d. The pale sky stretched thin over the angular skyline.
3. Sentences – fragments:	28	a. The sun climbing slowly into the morning sky. b. Wind blowing irresistibly through narrow alleys. c. Small waves lapping at the harbour wall. d. Diverse people lunching in the park.
4. Sentences – repetition:	29	Wind blowing high among flag poles and aerials; wind blowing low among waste bins and hydrants; wind scattering leaves in the parks; wind driving the spray from sprinklers onto roads and passing cars; wind flicking the coats and collars of pedestrians, who clasp their arms in front and push against the gales.
5. Descriptive figures – personifications:	29	a. The warm sun smiled gently on the children's cheeks. b. The smoke curled comfortingly around the ageing chimney. c. Two large windows silently stared across the harbour.
6. Descriptive figures – anachronisms:	29	a. So much leaf and shadow it would not be surprising to see an ancient sauropod munching on ferns between the trees. b. So much red dust in the street it would not be surprising to see a gang of bushrangers riding horses through the town. c. So much heraldry on the walls it would not be surprising to see knights in armour on their chargers, jousting in the courtyard.

Project 2: Write a story

Introduction

IN THIS SECTION:
- Preview the task

Many stories show a character undertaking a journey of some kind. A physical journey contains a lot of the ingredients needed for an exciting narrative. A journey has a beginning, an end, and a sequence of events. It also implies a goal, and obstacles that must be overcome. These are some of the basic elements of a dramatic plot.

A physical journey can also introduce symbolic elements into a story, enriching its meaning. We often speak of life as a journey. This idea makes the journey a useful symbol for change, growth and self-discovery. The connection between a physical journey and themes of self-discovery is a standard *motif* in literary fiction – that is, a standard recurring *pattern* or *structure* in storytelling.

In this project you will use a journey motif to tell a simple story from a child's point of view. You will also learn how to use contrasts and symbols to enrich the meaning of your tale.

Goal: Write a journey-based story that features a detailed setting, a plot inversion, and a powerful symbol.

Skills you will learn from this project:

- building a plot using a *journey format*
- describing a scene using *imagery*
- creating a dramatic contrast using *inversion*
- designing a complex *symbol*
- creating a colloquial style through *phrasing*
- using sentence length to control *pace*

Special terms: *inversion, periphrasis, parenthesis, prosopopoeia*

Step 1: The model

IN THIS SECTION:
- Read an example
- Explore its features and usage

In this project you will copy a story by the Swedish author, Pär Lagerkvist (1891-1974). Lagerkvist was a writer of essays, plays, stories and novels. His most famous novel, *Barabbas,* was made into a film in 1961. Lagerkvist's literary works often explore questions of good and evil. His stories frequently feature religious themes and powerful symbols.

Pär Lagerkvist won the Nobel Prize for Literature in 1951.

Before reading

The story "Father and I" is set in the Swedish countryside in about 1901. It tells of a father and son who take a walk into the woods one Sunday afternoon. During this ordinary journey, the boy gradually becomes aware of dangers that lie ahead in his life, and he is overcome by fear.

Read the story carefully, paying attention to the *stages of the journey* and the *contrasts* in the story.

Words to know:

anemone – a woodland flower, similar to a buttercup

meadowsweet – a type of wild rose that grows beside streams

crofter – a person who farms a very small field

platelayer – a worker who lays and repairs railway line

semaphore – a signalling system; in the story a railway post with lights or moving arms that signals train movements

sleepers – rectangular blocks used as a base for railway lines or tracks

balks – ridges of unploughed land

Father and I

1   When I was getting on toward ten, I remember, Father took me by the hand one Sunday afternoon, as we were to go out into the woods and listen to the birds singing. Waving goodbye to Mother, who had to stay at home and get the evening meal, we set off briskly in the warm sunshine. We didn't make any great-to-do about this going to listen to the
5   birds, as though it were something extra special or wonderful; we were sound, sensible people Father and I, brought up with nature and used to it. There was nothing to make a fuss about. It was just that it was Sunday afternoon and Father was free. We walked along the railway line where people were not allowed to go as a rule, but Father worked on the railway and so had a right to. By doing this we could get straight into the woods,
10 too, without going a roundabout way.

  Soon the bird song began and all the rest. There was a twittering of finches and willow warblers, thrushes and sparrows in the bushes, the hum that goes on all around you as soon as you enter a wood. The ground was white with wood anemones, the birches had just come out into leaf, and the spruces had fresh shoots; there were scents on all sides,
15 and underfoot the mossy earth lay steaming in the sun. There was noise and movement everywhere; bumble-bees came out of their holes, midges swarmed wherever it was marshy, and birds darted out of the bushes to catch them and back again as quickly.

  All at once a train came rushing along and we had to go down on to the embankment. Father hailed the engine driver with two fingers to his Sunday hat and the driver saluted
20 and extended his hand. It all happened quickly; then on we went, taking big strides so as to tread on the sleepers and not in the gravel, which was heavy going and rough on the shoes. The sleepers sweated tar in the heat, everything smelled, grease and meadowsweet, tar and heather by turns. The rails glinted in the sun. On either side of the line were telegraph poles, which sang as you passed them. Yes, it was a lovely day. The sky was
25 quite clear, not a cloud to be seen, and there couldn't be any, either, on a day like this, from what Father said.

  After a while we came to a field of oats to the right of the line, where a crofter we knew had a clearing. The oats had come up close and even. Father scanned them with an expert eye and I could see he was satisfied. I knew very little about such things, having been
30 born in a town. Then we came to the bridge over a stream, which most of the time had no water to speak of but which now was in full spate. We held hands so as not to fall down between the sleepers. After that it is not long before you come to the platelayer's cottage lying embedded in greenery, apple trees and gooseberry bushes. We called in to see them and were offered milk, and saw their pig and hens and fruit trees in blossom; then we
35 went on. We wanted to get to the river, for it was more beautiful there than anywhere

else; there was something special about it, as farther upstream it flowed past where Father had lived as a child. We usually liked to come as far as this before we turned back, and today, too, we got there after a good walk. It was near the next station, but we didn't go so far. Father just looked to see that the semaphore was right – he thought of everything.

40 We stopped by the river, which murmured in the hot sun, broad and friendly. The shady trees hung along the balks and were reflected in the backwater. It was all fresh and light here; a soft breeze was blowing off the small lakes higher up. We climbed down the slope and walked a little way along the bank, Father pointing out the spots for fishing. He had sat here on the stones as a boy, waiting for perch all day long; often there wasn't even a
45 bite, but it was a blissful life. Now he didn't have time. We hung about on the bank for a good while, making a noise, pushing out bits of bark for the current to take, throwing pebbles out into the water to see who could throw farthest; we were both happy and cheerful by nature, Father and I. At last we felt tired and that we had had enough, and we set off for home.

50 It was beginning to get dark. The woods were changed – it wasn't dark there yet, but almost. We quickened our steps. Mother would be getting anxious and waiting with supper. She was always afraid something was going to happen. But it hadn't; it had been a lovely day, nothing had happened that shouldn't. We were content with everything.

The twilight deepened. The trees were so funny. They stood listening to every step we
55 took as if they didn't know who we were. Under one of them was a glow-worm. It lay down there in the dark staring at us. I squeezed Father's hand, but he didn't see the strange glow, just walked on. Now it was quite dark. We came to the bridge over the stream. It roared down there in the depths, horribly, as though it wanted to swallow us up; the abyss yawned below us. We trod carefully on the sleepers, holding each other
60 tightly by the hand so as not to fall in. I thought Father would carry me across, but he didn't say anything; he probably wanted me to be like him and think nothing of it. We went on. Father was so calm as he walked there in the darkness, with even strides, not speaking, thinking to himself. I couldn't understand how he could be so calm when it was so murky. I looked all around me in fear. Nothing but darkness everywhere. I hardly
65 dared take a deep breath, for then you got so much darkness inside you, and that was dangerous. I thought it meant you would soon die. I remember quite well that's what I thought then. The embankment sloped steeply down as though into chasms black as night. The telegraph poles rose, ghostly, to the sky. Inside them was a hollow rumble as though someone were talking deep down in the earth and the white porcelain caps sat
70 huddled fearfully together listening to it. It was all horrible. Nothing was right, nothing real; it was all so weird.

Hugging close to Father, I whispered, "Father why is it so horrible when it's dark?"
"No my boy, it's not horrible," he said, taking me by the hand.
"Yes, Father it is."
75 "No, my child, you mustn't think that. Not when we know there is a God."

I felt so lonely, forsaken. It was so strange that only I was afraid, not Father, that we didn't think the same. And strange that what he said didn't help me and stop me from being afraid. Not even what he said about God helped me. I thought he too was horrible. It was horrible that he was everywhere here in the darkness, down under the trees, in the
80 telegraph poles which rumbled – that must be he – everywhere. And yet you could never see him.

We walked in silence, each with his own thoughts. My heart contracted as though the darkness had got in and was beginning to squeeze it.

Then, as we were rounding a bend we suddenly heard a mighty roar behind us! We were
85 awakened out of our thoughts in alarm. Father pulled me down on to the embankment, down into the abyss, held me there. Then the train tore past, a black train. All the lights in the carriages were out and it was going at frantic speed. What sort of train was it? There wasn't one due now! We gazed at it in terror. The fire blazed in the huge engine as they shovelled in coal; sparks whirled out into the night. It was terrible. The driver stood there
90 in the light of the fire, pale, motionless, his features as though turned to stone. Father didn't recognize him, didn't know who he was. The man just stared straight ahead, as though intent only on rushing into the darkness, far into the darkness that had no end.

Beside myself with dread, I stood there panting, gazing after the furious vision. It was swallowed up by the night. Father took me up on to the line; we hurried home. He said,
95 "Strange, what train was that? And I didn't recognize the driver." Then we walked on in silence.

But my whole body was shaking. It was for me, for my sake. I sensed what it meant: it was the anguish that was to come, the unknown, all that Father knew nothing about, that he wouldn't be able to protect me against. That was how this world, this life would be for me;
100 not like Father's, where everything was secure and certain. It wasn't a real world, a real life. It just hurtled, blazing, into the darkness that had no end.

Pär Lagerkvist
Translated by Alan Blair

After reading

The journey in "Father and I" has two clear stages. It is pleasant at first, but then becomes frightening. The writer creates the two stages by changing the setting from day to night. He also uses contrasting descriptions of objects and places such as the woodland trees and the telegraph poles. At first the objects seem familiar and friendly, but at night they become strange and sinister. Such a dramatic reversal in the mood and direction of a story is called an *inversion*.

The physical journey is also a *symbol of discovery* for the main character. The young boy sets out on the walk feeling confident that the world is a friendly place and that his father knows everything. But his experiences on the journey turn the boy's view of things upside down. The world becomes chaotic and hostile, and the boy worries that his father cannot protect him from it. He is left with a sense of dread about his future. The feeling of dread is reinforced by the rushing black train, a powerful symbol of the boy's fears.

Activity 1

1. Go back to the story and find the line numbers where the following occur.

Features of the story	Lines
a. Two clues that the story is being narrated by an adult, not a child.	
b. A "turning point" in the story, where the journey is reversed.	
c. An object described in contrasting ways – first as innocent, then as threatening.	
d. A statement declaring what the boy has learned from his journey.	

2. The two halves of the story develop different ideas about the world. Which of the following describe the way the ideas change? (Tick your choices.)

a. From order to chaos ☐   e. From authority to anarchy ☐

b. From artificial to natural ☐   f. From innocence to knowledge ☐

c. From rural past to industrial future ☐   g. From belief to scepticism ☐

d. From reality to imagination ☐   h. From love to hate ☐

Choose two and explain to your group or class how the ideas are presented in the story.

What's the use?

Journey stories are often symbolic of personal or social experiences. The physical journey in a story might represent psychological growth for the main character, as it does in "Father and I". Or it might be a way of exploring ideas and values in a concrete way. In the famous story, *Heart of Darkness* by Joseph Conrad, a man's journey down the Congo River in Africa raises complex questions about civilisation and savagery. In the TV show, *Battlestar Galactica*, a journey across space is used to explore ideas about home and belonging, community, prejudice and discrimination. The physical journey provides a platform for exploring the issues by bringing the characters into contact with places, people and problems that challenge their view of the world.

A physical journey often involves travel from somewhere familiar to somewhere new or unknown. This makes the journey format useful for telling stories about change or discovery. A physical journey often represents a life-change for the main character – from childhood to adulthood, or ignorance to knowledge. Most people can recall times in their childhood when they made great discoveries about the world and their place in it. Presenting such a discovery in the form of a journey turns a personal memory into a story that others can relate to.

The journey in a story can be simple or complex, short or long. A day trip to the zoo is a journey, but so is a round-the-world tour. This variety makes the journey a useful *motif* in many forms of writing, from short anecdotes and children's stories, to complex novels and feature films.

Learning to use the journey format in these ways will add depth and artistry to your stories, making them more satisfying for your readers.

Activity 2

1. "Father and I" tells of a small boy's discovery that the world can be frightening and that his father will not always be able to protect him from it.

    Here are some other familiar childhood "discoveries". Discuss the items and select *two* that you think could effectively be told as journeys.

    a. *Discovery:* The world is larger than your home street.

    b. *Discovery:* People can be cruel.

    c. *Discovery:* People have different ways of living.

    d. *Discovery:* Strangers can be kind.

2. Here is a suggested journey story for one of the "discoveries" listed above.

Discovery: The world is larger than your home street.

Story: An older cousin takes a young child riding on his new bike; the child enjoys the ride but panics when he realises he can no longer see his house or anyone familiar – even though they have only ridden into the next street.

Write down how one other discovery could be told as a journey story. Share the ideas with members of your group or class.

Discovery: ....

Story: ....

Now that you have read the story and discussed the use of journey narratives, you have a goal for your writing. Your aim will be to write a story that imitates the structure and style of "Father and I" by Pär Lagerkvist.

Step 2: Ideas and design

IN THIS SECTION:
- Learn to organise your ideas
- Learn to make a plan
- Write a first draft

Before you can learn to write a story like "Father and I", you need to study how the story is constructed. We will start our analysis by looking at the ideas and design of the story.

Ideas: characters, setting, symbol

For such a powerful story, "Father and I" is constructed from simple elements. The main ingredients are characters, setting and symbol.

Characters: traveller and guide

Like many journey-based stories, "Father and I" has two character types: a traveller and a guide. The guide is experienced and knowledgeable, while the traveller is inexperienced and trusting. An interesting feature of this particular story is that the character roles are almost reversed by the end of the tale. While the father seems powerful and all-knowing at the start of the journey, he seems less so at the end.

The story is told in *first person narration* by the traveller. This is common for journey stories, which almost always focus on the traveller rather than the guide. The narration includes two kinds of information.

1. *Observation and reporting:* The young traveller tells us about the people, places and events in the journey, and describes them for us. For example: "We set off briskly in the warm sunshine..." and "We walked along the railway line."

2. *Commentary on his feelings:* In addition to reporting the events of the journey, the boy also reports his feelings. For example: "I felt so lonely, forsaken..." and "Beside myself with dread, I stood there..."

In building your own story, you will need to include both kinds of information.

Remember that the narrator of the story is an adult looking back on events in his childhood. This means that the storyteller understands more about the events now than he did at the time. But he is careful not to let that knowledge intrude into the story. For the most part, he tells the story from the perspective of a ten year old.

Activity 3

1. Go back to the story and check for yourself how the roles of guide and traveller have been developed. Look for examples of the following. Note down where they occur.

Features of the story	Lines
a. Two statements that show the father as a knowledgeable guide	
b. Two statements that show the boy's inexperience and trust	
c. Two statements about objects and events in the story	
d. Two statements reporting the boy's thoughts and feelings	

2. Imagine that you are asked to write an extra scene for the story. Here are some sentences that could be included. Tick those you would choose. (*Remember:* The observations should be in the first person, from a child's perspective.)

   a. I always felt safe on these walks with father. ☐
   b. The green tendrils of a woodland creeper waved to me in the breeze. ☐
   c. My father feared crossing the bridge, worrying that I might slip and fall. ☐
   d. The father looked down at his son and smiled with pride. ☐
   e. The rushing water sounded like a mighty waterfall in the dark. ☐

3. What other combinations of guide and traveller could be used for a story like this? Add two more to the following suggestions:

   a. mother/daughter
   b. tribal elder/child
   c. youth leader/scout
   d. . . . . / . . . .
   e. . . . . / . . . .

Character: four rules

1. There are two character types: a traveller and a guide.

2. The guide is experienced and knowledgeable, while the traveller is inexperienced and trusting.

3. The story is told in the first person ("I") by the traveller.

4. The narrator gives two kinds of information: about people, places and events, and about his reactions and feelings.

Setting and inversion

The *setting* is the time and place where the journey takes place. In this story, the setting is a rural area of Sweden around 1901. The physical setting includes a woodland, a small field, a river, a bridge, and a railway line. These mark the stages of the journey, and each is described in detail. Sights, sounds and smells are all mentioned, creating a strong sensory impression.

The setting undergoes a dramatic reversal, or *inversion*, in the course of the journey. As day becomes night, the boy's perception of his surroundings changes. What at first appeared familiar and innocent soon seems strange and sinister. The reversal is so dramatic that the story can be divided into two distinct parts – one positive, the other negative. We can summarise the two parts as follows.

Outward journey (day)	Return journey (night)
The setting is familiar, friendly.	The setting is strange, sinister.
Descriptions emphasise life and non-living things.	Descriptions emphasise dangers and living things.
The guide is trusted.	The guide is questioned.
The outlook is optimistic.	The outlook is pessimistic.

In creating your story, you can choose any suitable setting. The important thing is to introduce a *dramatic inversion* that will reverse the reader's impression of the place and events.

Activity 4

1. Go back to the story and look at the change in setting, from positive to negative. Find:

   a. two statements that present the setting as familiar and friendly.
   b. two statements that present the setting as strange and sinister.

2. Where exactly does the "turning point" occur in the story?

   a. Mark the turning point using a ruled line, or other symbol.
   b. How close to the middle of the story is the turning point? (*Suggestion:* do a word-count.)

3. Here are some possible settings for a journey-based story. Add three more of your own. (*Suggestion:* consider your guide and traveller, and create a setting to match.)

   a. a trip to a big city   d. ....
   b. a river cruise   e. ....
   c. an aeroplane flight   f. ....

4. For each of the above, consider what kind of *inversion* you could introduce into the story. Add three more examples to the following list.

    a. From day to night

    b. From fine weather to storms

    c. From open space to enclosed

    d. From .... to ....

    e. From .... to ....

    f. From .... to ....

Setting: four rules

1. The setting contains physical features that mark the stages of the journey.
2. The physical aspects of each stage of the journey are described in detail.
3. Sights, sounds and smells are described in detail, creating a strong sensory impression for the reader.
4. The mood is dramatically reversed, or *inverted*, at a turning point in the story.

Symbol

"Father and I" is more than a simple anecdote about an afternoon walk. It also addresses larger themes. The young boy's fear of the dark woods can be read as an allegory about the anxieties of growing up. The story also can be read as a premonition of two events that would change rural life in Europe for ever – mechanisation and the First World War (1914–18). These ideas are conveyed partly through the literal events of the story and partly through well-chosen symbols.

A *symbol* is an image or object that stands for something else. Familiar symbols in daily life include giving of roses as a symbol of love, or wearing a ring as a symbol of commitment. Literary symbols are usually more complicated than this. The main symbol in "Father and I" is the rushing black train that appears in the story, with its flashing sparks and strangely inhuman driver. This larger-than-life image of a steam train, out of control, stands for the frightening future that lies ahead for the young boy.

The narrator of the story openly encourages us to view the train as a symbol. He says:

"It was for me, for my sake. I sensed what it meant: it was the anguish that was to come."

For an image to work effectively as a symbol it must have four features:

1. *Relevance:* The object must fit into the scene and be believable in the setting. The train fits into the scene because steam trains were an important form of transport in 1901, and because the characters are walking along a railway line. An alien spaceship would not be as relevant or believable.

2. *Significance:* The object must stand out. It will not work as a symbol if it blends in with other physical features of the setting. A writer can draw attention to a symbol in a number of ways: through repetition, or contrast, or by the intensity of its description. The black train gains symbolic power because it is a contrast to the first train and because it is a powerful visual image. The writer uses strong, active verbs to emphasise the train's appearance and action: "the fire *blazed*", "sparks *whirled*", the train was "*rushing* into the darkness".

3. *Connotation:* The object's physical properties must convey the right feelings and associations. The train has a number of features that make it suitable as a symbol of fear and death: it is black, it is fiery, its driver is stony-faced, it is mechanical (in contrast to the living landscape). A herd of wild deer could also frighten the travellers, but it would not have the same connotations of death and inhuman coldness.

4. *Ambiguity:* A symbol often works best when it implies more than one meaning. If the black train had a German Iron Cross painted on its side, there would be no question that it symbolised the coming war; but its power as a symbol would then be reduced. It would be more like a cartoonist's caricature than a true symbol. Some degree of ambiguity is more satisfying for readers.

Balancing these features can be difficult. That is what makes symbol such a complex technique to use in your writing.

Activity 5

1. Imagine a child taking her first journey by aeroplane.

   a. The first half of the journey is by day, in sunny weather. The child is filled with joy.
   b. The return journey is by night, in rain and storms. The child is filled with fear.

   Which of the short scenarios, listed on the next page, could serve as a useful *symbol* for the child's fear during the return journey?

Rank the scenarios from best (1) to worst (5), considering the four rules of relevance, significance, connotation and ambiguity.

Scenarios	Ranking
a. A dark thundercloud filled with strange green lightning appears; the plane flies into the cloud and shakes violently as the lightning and thunder crash around it.	
b. Another aeroplane appears in the distance and roars past, far too close, frightening the passengers.	
c. A long dormant volcano erupts below the plane and spews hot ash into the air, momentarily stalling the engines.	
d. An unexplained light follows the plane, and the cabin is filled with a bright glare, and people's watches and clocks run backwards.	
e. A blast of turbulence rocks the cabin, and a crucifix slips from an overhead locker, dangling in front of the young child as the plane lurches and shakes.	

Discuss the reasons for your choices.

2. Here are two more suggestions for journey stories. What *symbols* could be used in the stories to represent the challenges and dangers of life?

   a. A father and son go on a bushwalking expedition.
   b. An uncle and nephew take a trip to the city.

Choose from the following, or suggest your own: Story a.   Story b.

   a. a steep slope with thorny bushes   ☐   ☐
   b. a flash flood that nearly drowns the walkers   ☐   ☐
   c. a truck that almost runs down the characters   ☐   ☐
   d. a grove of dead trees infested with reptiles   ☐   ☐
   e. an aggressive and abusive passerby   ☐   ☐
   f. a freeway filled with traffic   ☐   ☐

Writing a symbol: four rules
1. *Relevance:* the object should match the time, place and events of the narrative.
2. *Significance:* the object should catch the reader's attention, through repetition, contrast or emphasis.
3. *Connotation:* the object should convey the right feelings and associations.
4. *Ambiguity:* the object should be open to interpretation rather than highly specific.

Design: journey structure, inversion

Journey stories can be linear or circular in structure. In a linear story, the travellers follow a path that takes them from one location to another, where the story ends. In a circular story, the journey takes the travellers to a distant location and back again.

Circular design
Pär Lagerkvist's story uses the circular design.

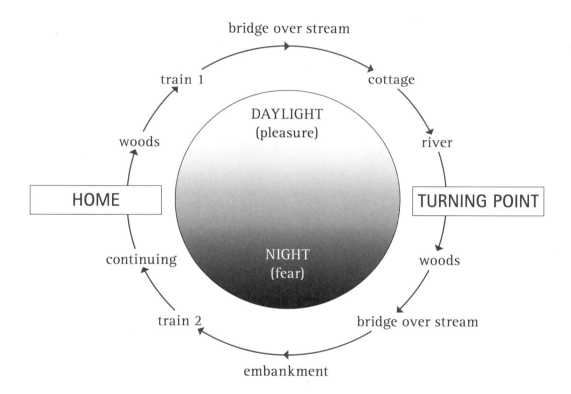

The two halves of the story have been carefully balanced. The length of each is almost exactly the same, and many of the objects and events from the first half are repeated in the second half – though in an inverted (reverse) form.

Detailed structure

The detailed structure of the story can be shown like this. The journey is broken into stages, and each stage introduces new objects, events and people. The table below shows how the first part of the story is structured.

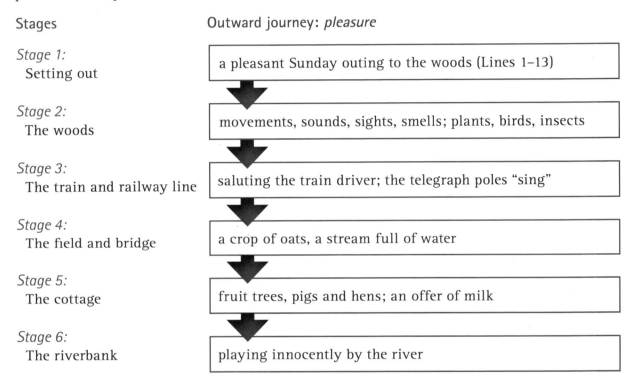

Stages   Outward journey: *pleasure*

Stage 1:
  Setting out

a pleasant Sunday outing to the woods (Lines 1–13)

Stage 2:
  The woods

movements, sounds, sights, smells; plants, birds, insects

Stage 3:
  The train and railway line

saluting the train driver; the telegraph poles "sing"

Stage 4:
  The field and bridge

a crop of oats, a stream full of water

Stage 5:
  The cottage

fruit trees, pigs and hens; an offer of milk

Stage 6:
  The riverbank

playing innocently by the river

Turning point: *from day to night and from pleasure to fear*

Activity 6

1.   a.   Go back to the story on pages 39–41 and number each of the stages shown above, pinpointing in the margin where each section occurs.

       b.   Then record the line numbers for each stage. The line numbers for the first stage have been filled in as an example.

2.   On the next page there is a chart showing the stages of the *second* part of the story, which takes place after the inversion or turning point in the story.

       a.   Go back to the story on pages 39–41 and find where each section occurs.

       b.   Make brief notes about each stage of the story, following the examples on the chart above.

Stages	Return journey: *fear*
Stage 7: The woods	
Stage 8: The bridge and stream	
Stage 9: The embankment	
Stage 10: The black train	
Stage 11: Continuing towards home	
Stage 12: The conclusion	

3. When you have completed your notes on stages 7 to 12 compare them with stages 1 to 6. What differences or *inversions* do you notice between the two halves of the story?

4. Below are brief descriptions of objects and events experienced by the travellers during different stages of the journey. Assign each to either the first (1) or second (2) part of the story.

a. The time is day.		k. The stream roars "horribly".	
b. There is a scent of "tar and heather".		l. The trees are leafy and beautiful.	
c. The train is "terrible" and strange.		m. The people they meet are friendly.	
d. The "ghostly" telegraph poles rumble.		n. Anemones carpet the ground.	
e. It is deepening twilight.		o. The rails glint in the sun.	
f. The father doesn't see what lies ahead.		p. The trees are sinister.	
g. The train travels at a "frantic" speed.		q. The telegraph poles sing.	
h. The glow-worm gives off a "strange glow".		r. The train driver waves.	
i. The father is knowledgeable.		s. The train driver is pale, motionless.	
j. The boy sees the darkness ahead.		t. The stream is in full spate.	

Building the scenario

You now understand the ideas and structure of the story, "Father and I", well enough to start planning your own narrative. Below are two scenarios ("scene summaries") that could be used as starting points for a similar story.

Scenario 1

Traveller and guide:	mother and daughter
Journey setting:	an aeroplane flight
Inversion:	daytime, fine weather / night time, storms
Symbol:	a large thundercloud that shakes the plane violently

Scenario 2

Traveller and guide:	uncle and nephew
Journey setting:	a trip to the city by bus and ferry
Inversion:	morning, calm and cool / afternoon, frenzied and hot
Symbol:	a rushing van that nearly runs the nephew over

Activity 7

1. Using ideas from the previous activities, develop two more scenarios like the ones above.

2. Share your ideas with others in your group or class. You should be able to build at least 10 different scenarios for writing.

Stages and details

To make the physical aspects of the journey convincing, you will need to plan *stages* and provide *details* about the objects and events that the travellers encounter.

The *stages* are places that the travellers pass through. In "Father and I", the stages include: woods, railway line, fields, cottage and so on.

The *details* are the objects and events that occur within each stage. In "Father and I", the detailed descriptions include sights, sounds and smells. For example: "twittering of finches and willow warblers"; "underfoot the mossy earth lay steaming"; "the ground was white with wood anemones"; "midges swarmed"; "birds darted"; "everything smelled, grease and meadowsweet, tar and heather in turn."

Activity 8

1. Consider the story scenario of an aeroplane flight with six stages on the *outward journey*, which takes place on *a fine day*. Tick the details below that you would choose to include.

Stages	Details
1. The take off	☐ a. the exciting roar of the engines
	☐ b. the giddy feel of take-off as the ground races away
2. Flying over land	☐ c. a fairground below, with slowly turning ferris wheel
	☐ d. mother calmly reading
3. Inside the cabin	☐ e. a bright red scarf on the neck of a stewardess
	☐ f. tiny cars on a freeway like shiny coloured beads
4. Crossing the coast	☐ g. soft white clouds like spun sugar
	☐ h. people talking and laughing in the sunlit cabin
5. Over the ocean	☐ i. a greasy haze of smog on the horizon
	☐ j. mother smiling and joking with the lunch stewards
6. The landing	☐ k. flecks of white in the blue ocean far below
	☐ l. the whine and thud of some hidden machinery

2. Suggest three more details you could add. (Consider things seen inside and outside the 'plane.)

3. Now consider the *return journey*, which takes place on *a stormy night*. Here are details that could be used. Some of these are inversions of descriptions above. Add three more details.

    a. the howling of the engines
    b. blackness outside, as if someone had painted over the windows
    c. a disorienting queasiness as the aeroplane floated upward
    d. the deep ocean far below, blackly invisible
    e. morbid silence in the dimly lit cabin
    f. mother staring at her book, but not turning the pages
    g. a sharp electrical smell in the cabin

Planning your own story

Now that you have developed some scenarios and details, you are ready to plan your story. For your first attempt, you will use the scenario of the aeroplane journey.

Activity 9

1. Complete the blank sections of the plan on the next page, in note form only. You can use the notes and ideas from the activities you have completed above.

Plan for a story – using journey motif, inversion and symbol

Ideas

Traveller and guide:	mother and daughter
Journey setting:	an aeroplane flight
Inversion:	daytime, fine weather / night time, storms
Symbol:	a storm cloud that shakes the plane violently

Write down other ideas: ....

....

Design

Stages	Outward journey: *pleasure*
Note down some of the details you will include in each stage of the outward journey.	
Stage 1: Taking off during the day –	
Stage 2: Flying over land –	
Stage 3: Inside the cabin –	
Stage 4: Crossing the coast –	
Stage 5: Over the ocean –	
Stage 6: The landing –	

Turning point – from day to night; fine to storms

Stages	Return journey: *fear*
Note down some of the details you will include in each stage of the return journey.	
Stage 7: Taking off at night –	
Stage 8: Inside the cabin –	
Stage 9: Over the ocean –	
Stage 10: The storm cloud –	
Stage 11: The landing –	
Stage 12: The conclusion –	

2. Once you have made your plan, go on and write the first draft of your story. Do your best to imitate the design and writing style of "Father and I". You may like to use some of the following sentences to get started, and at different points in your story.

When I was about eleven my mother took me on a day flight to another city for one of her business meetings..."

"Soon the normal routine of the flight began in the cabin..."

"I peered at the ocean far below and saw the white flecks of waves on its blue surface..."

"It was already night as we prepared for our return flight, and the weather was turning bad. It all seemed very different in the dark..."

"Mother was staring intently at her book, but she wasn't turning the pages..."

"The deep ocean far below was blackly invisible. I felt it wanted to swallow me up..."

"I knew what it meant..."

> Put your draft to one side when you are finished. Don't worry if it is not yet very polished. You will return to it as you work through the following section on style.

Copying or dictation

Study closely the first five lines of the story on page 39. Pay attention to these things:

1. The length and wording of the sentences

2. The punctuation used

3. The spelling (especially the spelling of unfamiliar words)

Copy the paragraph into your notebook, checking against the original as you go. Make sure you capture the wording and punctuation exactly. Alternatively, write out the lines as your teacher reads them aloud. When you are done, discuss any features of the writing that have come to your attention.

Step 3: Style

IN THIS SECTION:
- Learn the writer's techniques
- Study diction, sentences, and special features
- Improve your draft in stages

Now that you understand the overall design of Pär Lagerkvist's story, it is time to examine the style – that is, the way words and sentences are used in the writing. The activities that follow will help you learn about three main aspects of the style: *diction, sentence patterns* and *descriptions.*

Diction

The term *diction* refers to the words that are used in the writing. The choice and arrangement of words will have a powerful effect on your reader. It is one of the main tools for shaping the tone and style of your story.

Compare these two paragraphs.

Paragraph A: When I was getting on toward ten, I remember, Father took me by the hand one Sunday afternoon as we were to go out into the woods and listen to the birds singing. We didn't make any great-to-do about this going to listen to the birds, as though it were something extra special or wonderful; we were sound, sensible people Father and I, brought up with nature and used to it.

Paragraph B: When I was almost ten, Father took me to the woods one Sunday afternoon to listen to the birds singing. It wasn't a special occasion; we were not sentimental about nature. We were sensible people.

These two short paragraphs say much the same thing, but they create quite different effects for the reader.

Paragraph A seems informal, casual and friendly – more like spoken language than writing. It also seems unhurried, as if the storyteller is not in a rush.

Paragraph B is shorter and sharper. It conveys the facts in a more detached, impersonal manner. These differences are the result of word choice and arrangement. For example, "getting on toward ten", is more casual and wordy than "almost ten". Such casual wordiness is a feature of *colloquial* style.

Colloquial style

Pär Lagerkvist has written his story in a style that is *colloquial* and *subjective*.

Colloquial means "conversational" – the style in which people commonly speak.

Subjective means "personal".

A story written in colloquial style sounds as if it is being told aloud, and emphasises the personal feelings and reactions of the storyteller.

Lagerkvist's subjective, colloquial style has three important features:

1. *Concrete nouns, with adjectives for feelings:* The story is full of concrete nouns that refer to aspects of the journey, such as "oats", "sleepers", "finches". Most of the nouns stand alone, without description. The few adjectives used are simple: for example, "*white* anemones", "*hot* sun". The exception is that there are many adjectives used to describe feelings: for example, "happy", "cheerful", "lonely", "forsaken".

2. *First person pronouns and parenthesis.* The story contains many uses of the pronouns "I" and "we". It also contains many short phrases that refer to the storyteller's feelings or thought processes. For example: "I remember", "we thought", "I recall now", "I felt", "I believe". These subjective phrases *interrupt* the main sentence. For example: "When I was getting on toward ten, *I remember,* Father took me by the hand." This kind of interruption is called *parenthesis* (which means "placing alongside").

3. *Homely phrases, periphrasis.* The writer often uses phrases in place of single words. For example, "getting on toward ten", instead of "almost ten". These phrases have a homely quality, and because they are wordy they create an impression that the narrator is not in a hurry. The result is a relaxed, friendly style. Wordy phrases are a form of *periphrasis*, which means talking in a roundabout way. Other examples are "bird song *and all the rest*"; "the hum that *goes on all around you*"; "had no water *to speak of*".

Activity 10

1. Read the opening paragraphs again of the story on page 39 and underline examples of:

   a. concrete nouns (e.g. "finches", "oats") and simple adjectives (e.g. "white", "hot").

   b. adjectives that describe feelings (e.g. "happy", "sad").

   c. first person pronouns (e.g. "I", "we") and subjective parentheses (e.g. "I felt").

   d. periphrasis; i.e. indirect phrasing and wordiness (e.g. "getting on toward").

2. To test if the style remains the same throughout the story, you can perform a simple counting analysis. Compare two paragraphs from different parts of the story and use the following table to record some features of the language in each. (A more complete table is on page 148.)

Number of concrete nouns (e.g. stone, rain, bread, mud)		
Number of adjectives for objects (e.g. white anemone, hot sun)		
Number of adjectives for feelings (e.g. happy, sad)		
Number of personal pronouns (e.g. I, we)		
Number of subjective parentheses (e.g. I remember)		

3. Change the following sentences so that they match the style of "Father and I".

    Periphrasis: add "homely" phrases in place of the underlined words.

    a. We caught the plane at <u>exactly</u> 10.00am.

    ....

    b. When we <u>approached</u> the airport, people fastened their belts.

    ....

    c. We were late and my Dad would be <u>anxious.</u>

    ....

    Subjective parenthesis: add "interrupting" phrases using "I" or "we", at the place shown (//). (Use commas to separate your interruptions from the main sentence.)

    d. It was my first flight // and I was excited.

    ....

    e. I wasn't the least bit nervous //.

    ....

    f. We were both calm by nature // so the noises didn't concern us.

    ....

> Go back to your draft and check that your style is colloquial and subjective. Look for where you can use personal pronouns, subjective interruptions, and homely phrases.

Diction: four rules

1. The setting is described through concrete nouns. Adjectives are used to describe feelings.

2. The narrator's thoughts are recorded in short first-person phrases (e.g. "I remember", "I felt").

3. Homely phrases ("getting on toward ten") are used instead of single words to create a leisurely, relaxed and friendly style.

4. Vivid images are used to appeal to the reader's senses of sight, smell, sound, touch, and taste.

Images

Pär Lagerkvist's story features many vivid descriptions of things the boy and his father encounter on their journey. These descriptions create strong sense impressions called *images*. Images help the reader imagine the setting, by appealing to the familiar senses of sight, smell, touch, taste and sound.

Activity 11

1. Go back to the story on page 39 and find examples of the following. (Jot down the line numbers where they occur.)

   a. a description of something seen
   b. a description of something heard
   c. a description of something smelled or tasted
   d. a description of something touched

2. Which of the five senses is used most often in the story? Which is used least often?

3. Check your own story draft for sensory images. Can you find:

   a. a description of something seen?
   b. a description of something heard?
   c. a description of something smelled or tasted?
   d. a description of something touched?

Inversion and contrast

One of the most interesting features of "Father and I" is the way descriptions are *inverted* to create a dramatic contrast between the two halves of the story. Things that seem pleasant in the first part of the story become sinister toward the end.

Compare these two descriptions of the sound made by the telegraph poles.

> On either side of the railway line were telegraph poles, *which sang as you passed them.*

> The telegraph poles rose, ghostly, to the sky. *Inside them was a hollow rumble* as though someone was talking deep down in the earth.

Although the two sentences describe the same object (a telegraph pole), they give it very different characteristics. *Inversions* like this have been used throughout the story.

The contrasting descriptions in the story are created in three main ways.

1. *Inverting the imagery:* The images in each part of the story follow a pattern, called a *motif.* Images in the first half of the story all create an impression of *life and movement.* For example: "birds and insects swarming"; "the running stream"; "fruit trees in blossom". Images in the second half of the story create an impression of *decay, death and danger.* For example: "the glow worm in the dark"; "the deep chasm under the bridge"; "the black train".

2. *Changing the connotations:* Some descriptions in the story have been *inverted* through a change of words. In the first part of the story, the telegraph poles "sing". In the second part of the story, they "rumble". In the first part of the story, the stream runs "in full spate". In the second part it "roars below". These changes in wording create different *connotations* – that is, different emotional effects – that reinforce the inversion.

3. *Personification:* Many descriptions in the story use personification, or *prosopopoeia.* This means describing non-living things as if they have the qualities of persons or animals. (The term *prosopopoeia* literally means "giving a face" to something.) Examples include: "the telegraph poles sang"; "the river murmured". These descriptions work by using a verb that is normally associated with human action.

Creating contrasting descriptions: three rules

  1. Create a pattern of images that can be inverted.

  2. Change words to form contrasts.

  3. Use personified verbs (e.g. "the river *murmured*").

Activity 12

1. Go back to the story and underline examples of the following features:

   a. images that suggest life and movement

   b. images that suggest death, decay or danger

   c. changes in wording and connotation

   d. examples of personification

2. Below are some short descriptions that could be inserted into the story "Father and I". Each item forms a pair of contrasting images.

   Complete the descriptions by choosing from the words and phrases below the chart.

Object	Image 1 (positive)	Image 2 (negative)
a. *A vine*	Young green .... brushed my skin.	Clinging .... grabbed at me in the darkness.
b. *A path*	A tree-lined path opened before us like a	The path was like a .... in which I might be trapped.
c. *A cave*	A small cave .... cool air on us as we passed.	The cave mouth .... the night air, as if to draw us in.
d. *Insects*	Swarming midges .... in the air.	A cloud of bugs .... us.

   Choices: dark tunnel, breathed, danced, sunlit hallway, tendrils, smothered, tentacles, gulped

3. Find two examples of word change and personification in the above table.

> Go back to your draft and experiment with sensory images, connotation and personification to enhance the contrast in your story. Use two examples of each.

Sentence patterns

The sentences in Pär Lagerkvist's story have two interesting features.

1. *Structure:* The first interesting feature is their structure. Many of the sentences begin with a *consistent pattern* of words.

2. *Sentence length and pace:* The second interesting feature is the way the length of the sentences changes to create pace and tension.

Main subject openings

Many sentences in "Father and I" are simple statements that begin by putting the main subject first. The following examples all begin with the main subject, followed by a verb – that is, they begin with a person or thing who does something, or with a statement about the setting.

> *We walked* along the railway line...
>
> *Father hailed* the engine driver...
>
> *The ground was* white...
>
> *The oats had come up* close and even...

Putting the main subject first gives the sentences a simple, direct quality that matches the colloquial style of the storytelling.

Time and sequence openings

For variety, some sentences in the story use different kinds of opening. These alternative openings often refer to the timing and sequence of events. For example:

> *Soon* the bird song began...
>
> *At last* we felt tired...
>
> *All at once* a train came rushing...
>
> *After a while* we came to a field...

Some common phrases for time and sequence openings are: "soon", "before long", "eventually", "later", "not long after", "all of a sudden", "instantly", "in a flash", and so on.

Sentence structure: two rules

1. Simple statements that begin with the main subject of the sentence are used.

2. Some sentences open with a reference to the timing and sequence of events.

Activity 13

1. Go back to the story on pages 39–41 and underline the following.

   a. Four examples of sentences that begin with the main subject.
   b. Four examples of openings that tell the time or sequence of events.

2. Rewrite the following sentences into *main subject openings*. (The subjects are underlined.)

   a. Along the bank of the river <u>we</u> walked.
   b. The semaphore signals were something <u>father</u> understood.
   c. All through the woods, <u>birds</u> were calling.

3. Rewrite the following sentences into *time and sequence openings*.

   a. We came to a bend in river after a while.
   b. A black train suddenly emerged from a railway tunnel.
   c. The platelayer's cottage was our next stop.

> Go back to your draft and examine your sentences. Check that you have used a variety of main subject and time sequence openings in your story.

Sentence length and pace

Sentence length is an important aspect of style. It can be used to create many different effects.

Pär Lagerkvist has used sentence length to:

1. create *contrast*
2. change the *pace* in his story.

Pace is the rate at which things seem to happen in a narrative. Writers generally *increase* the pace when they want to create a sense of danger or excitement, as if things are spinning out of control. They *slow* the pace to create a sense of calm.

As a rule, short sentences increase the pace, while long sentences slow the pace.

We have seen that "Father and I" can be divided into two parts. The first half of the story conveys a sense of pleasure, the second conveys fear and danger. What can you predict about the length of sentences in each half?

Activity 14

1. Use the following table to analyse some features of the sentences in "Father and I".

Total number of sentences in the story	109
Length of longest sentence (i.e. number of words)	46
Length of shortest sentence (i.e. number of words)	
Number of sentences in the outward journey (paragraphs 1–5)	
Number of sentences in the return journey (paragraphs 6-12)	

2. Paragraphs five and six on page 40 are where the turning point occurs: where day turns to night and pleasure turns to fear. Study the sentences in the paragraphs and record your findings.

Paragraph five: "We stopped by the river..."

Number of sentences	
Number of words in each sentence (List them, e.g. 13 + 7 + ...)	
Total number of words	
Average sentence length for paragraph 5 (total words divided by number of sentences)	

Paragraph six: "It was beginning to get dark..."

Number of sentences	
Number of words in each sentence (List them, e.g. 13 + 7 + ...)	
Total number of words	
Average sentence length for paragraph 6 (total words divided by number of sentences)	

What do your findings reveal about the way sentence length has been used to control the pace?

> Go back to your draft and examine the length of sentences. Check you have used a shorter average sentence length in the second half of your story, to increase the pace. The average length of sentences in the first part should be about twice that of the second.

You have now finished revising your draft story.

Go to Step 4 on page 67 if you want more practice in colloquial diction, description and sentence style.

OR

Go straight to Step 5 on page 69 to write your final copy.

Step 4: Exercises (optional)

IN THIS SECTION:

■ Practise your new skills

Choose the skills that you need to practise, and complete the exercises for that topic.

1. *Diction:* Make these sentences more colloquial by adding homely phrases in place of the underlined words.

    a. We were cruising <u>barely</u> above the clouds.

    . . . .

    b. There were <u>exactly</u> five empty seats in the cabin.

    . . . .

    Insert subjective parentheses (I/we phrases) at the points shown (//).

    c. The flight was uneventful // until we crossed the coast.

    . . . .

    d. // The noise was so loud it seemed it would deafen me.

    . . . .

2. *Description and contrast:* Complete the following descriptions so that they form contrasting pairs. Choose from the words below.

Image 1 *(positive)*	Image 2 *(negative)*
a. The engines . . . . with power.	The engines . . . . in the darkness.
b. The tower lights . . . . in the sunlight.	A red beacon . . . . in the blackness below.
c. The cabin . . . . of hot food and steam.	The cabin . . . . of sweat and ozone.
d. The window glass felt . . . . on my cheek.	The seat buckle was . . . . on my hand.

Choices: cool, howled, winked, smelled, roared, stank, icy, pulsed

3. *Sentence length – increasing the pace:* Break each of the following into three shorter sentences, to increase the pace. (You may need to change the wording slightly.)

   a. The wing tilted up abruptly, the aeroplane banked left, and everyone on board was suddenly silent.

   ....

   b. It began to get dark and the clouds became grey as we climbed; Mother and I looked out at the coming night.

   ....

   c. We passed low over a light tower, the beacon pulsing in the dark below, and red light soaked the cabin.

   ....

4. *Sentence length – slowing the pace:* Change each of the following into one long sentence, to slow the pace. (You may need to change the wording.)

   a. A river meandered far below. It was like a silver thread. It ran through a patchwork of fields.

   ....

   b. There was a rustle of movement. Passengers unclipped their seatbelts and stretched. They reached for earphones and magazines.

   ....

   c. Outside were clouds. They slid calmly by. We hovered far above.

   ....

Step 5: The final copy

IN THIS SECTION:
- Put it all together
- Write the final copy
- Hand it in

Now you are ready to write the final version of your story. You should aim to match the design and style of "Father and I". On page 71 is a checklist you can use to assess your work.

Summary: Formula for a story using a journey motif, inversion and symbol

Purpose

To present a story about change or discovery, from a child or stranger's perspective.

Ideas

- Begin with a traveller, a guide, and a setting.

- Choose an *inversion* (e.g. day/night) to create contrast:
  - Part A: create a sense of pleasure.
  - Part B: create a sense of fear or danger.

- Select a *symbol* to represent the traveller's fear or excitement.
  - Remember: *relevance, significance, connotation, ambiguity.*

Design

- Develop stages for the journey, using landmarks:
  - Develop details for each stage.
  - Include the outward journey and the return.

Style

- Imitate Lagerkvist's colloquial style:
  - *Diction* – use simple diction; adjectives for feeling; homely phrases.
  - *Pronouns* – use first person pronouns (*I/we*) and subjective parentheses (e.g. *I recall*).
  - *Imagery* – for strong imagery, use sense-descriptions (*see, hear, touch, taste, smell*).
  - *Sentence structure* – use a combination of main subject and time-sequence sentence openings (e.g. *We walked on....; Shortly after....*).
  - *Sentence length* – vary sentence length in each half to change the pace (ratio of 2:1).

Going further

IN THIS SECTION:
- Get ideas for further writing

1. Think of a change or discovery in your own life, and create a journey story about it. Use the techniques you have learned, and follow the steps outlined in the formula on page 69.

2. Pär Lagerkvist's story structure can be used in reverse. A frightening walk into stormy woods could become pleasurable when the sun appears, giving the story a happy and optimistic ending. Write (or rewrite) a story using this reversed structure.

3. Collect examples of other journey narratives that you know. Consider stories, television shows, movies and computer games. Write a brief annotation for each one, as follows.

    a. Name the main traveller(s) and guide(s).

    b. Describe the setting and its obstacles.

    c. State whether the narrative is linear or circular.

    d. State whether the story contains an inversion.

    e. Identify any symbols in the story, and state their meaning.

4. Write a short journey narrative based on characters and situations from one of the stories you have collected. Use the format and techniques you have learned in this chapter.

5. Journey stories are often symbolic of wider personal or social experiences. Choose a journey narrative you admire and write a report on it that considers the kind of journey that is undertaken by the protagonist and what it might symbolise.

    (*Suggestions: Alice's Adventures in Wonderland; The Odyssey; Gulliver's Travels; Heart of Darkness; Journey to the Centre of the Earth; The Incredible Journey; Through the Tunnel; Star Trek: Voyager; Battlestar Galactica; The Straight Story; Zen and the Art of Motorcycle Maintenance.*)

Assessment checklist: Project 2

Score your work as follows: 2 points for each *Yes;* 1 point for *Partly*; 0 points for each *No.* Add the scores for a mark out of 20.

Project 2: Write a Story using a journey motif, inversion and symbol	
Ideas	**Tick the box**
Is there a clear theme of change or discovery on the journey?	No ☐ Partly ☐ Yes ☐
Is there an effective thematic inversion (e.g. from pleasure to fear)?	No ☐ Partly ☐ Yes ☐
Is there a clear and effective use of symbol? (Consider: relevance, significance, connotation, ambiguity.)	No ☐ Partly ☐ Yes ☐
Design	
Are the outward and return parts evenly balanced, with contrasting moods?	No ☐ Partly ☐ Yes ☐
Are there effective stages and details in the journey?	No ☐ Partly ☐ Yes ☐
Style	
Is the colloquial style effective? (Consider: use of first person pronouns, homely phrases, description of feelings, parentheses)	No ☐ Partly ☐ Yes ☐
Are there clear and strong sensory images? (Descriptions of things seen, touched, heard, tasted, smelled.)	No ☐ Partly ☐ Yes ☐
Is there effective inversion of the images? (e.g. from order to chaos; from safety to danger.)	No ☐ Partly ☐ Yes ☐
Are shorter sentences used to increase pace? (Is the ratio of length about 2:1?)	No ☐ Partly ☐ Yes ☐
Spelling and punctuation	
Are all of the words spelled correctly? Have commas been used correctly to separate parentheses?	No ☐ Partly ☐ Yes ☐
Comment:	
Date:	Score:

Quiz: Project 2

1. State three facts about author, Pär Lagerkvist.

   ....

2. What is a symbol, in literature? Give an example.

   ....

3. State four qualities that make a symbol effective.

   ....

4. What is a narrative inversion? Give two examples.

   ....

5. What is the difference between linear and circular narrative?

   ....

6. Explain the concept of pace, and describe how it can be controlled in a story.

   ....

7. State three characteristics of a colloquial style.

   ....

8. Give the meaning of the words *connotation* and *motif.*

   ....

9. Explain the terms: *periphrasis* and *parenthesis*, giving examples.

   ....

10. Give the meaning of *anemone, platelayer, crofter.*

    ....

Answers for Project 2 Activities

These are suggested answers. In some cases your wording may differ slightly. If in doubt, check with your teacher.

Activity	Page	Answers
1	42	1. a. paragraphs 1 and 6 contain clues (see Lines 1 & 52). See also Lines 60, 75 etc. b. The line "It was beginning to get dark" is the turning point (Line 50). c. The telegraph poles are innocent then threatening (Lines 24 & 68). d. The last paragraph tells what the boy discovered (see especially Lines 99–100). 2. a, c, d, e, f, g and h. are possible readings. b. is the reverse of the story's structure.
2	43–44	1. All could be told as journeys. 2. For discussion.
3	46	1. There are several references (a. See, for example, Lines 9–10; 26; 28–9; 39; 43 etc. b. See Lines 1; 29; 39; 56 etc. c. See Lines 11–17 etc. d. see Line 76 etc.). Check with your teacher. 2. a, b. and e. would all fit. c. is wrong because it introduces an adult perspective out of step with the narrative. d. is wrong because it changes the narrative point of view to third person. 3. Check with your teacher.
4	47–8	1. See: Pleasant – Lines 11–17; 22–26. Unpleasant – Lines 54–55; 68–71 etc. Discuss with your teacher. 2. a. The line "It was beginning to get dark" is the turning point. b. The turning point is in the middle. There are 799 words before it, and 782 after. 3. Check with your teacher. 4. Check with your teacher.
5	49	1. a. and e. are the best options. b. is not ambiguous. c. is not credible in the context. d. introduces a paranormal element inconsistent with the realism of the story genre. 2. Discuss the options with your teacher.
6	52	1. This is a self-checking task. 2. and 3. Check with your teacher. 4. a, b, i, l, m, n, o, q, r, t occur in the first half of the story. The rest are in the second.
7	54	Check with your teacher.
8	55	1, 2. and 3. Check with your teacher.
9	55	This is a self-checking task.

Activity	Page	Answers
10	59–60	1. Check with your teacher. 2. This is a self-checking task. 3. a. We caught the plane right on 10.00am (or similar phrase). 　 b. When we got near to the airport (or similar phrase). 　 c. We were late and my Dad would be starting to worry (or similar phrase). 　 d. It was my first flight, I remember, and I was excited (or similar phrase). 　 e. I wasn't the least bit nervous, I recall (or similar phrase). 　 f. We were both calm by nature, mother and I, so the noises didn't concern us (or similar phrase).
11	61	1. This is a self-checking task. 2. Visual images are most common. Taste is not used. 3. This is a self-checking task.
12	63	1. Check with your teacher. 2. a. tendrils, tentacles 　 b. sunlit hallway, dark tunnel 　 c. breathed, gulped 　 d. danced, smothered 3. All examples contain word changes. Examples a. and c. contain personification.
13	65	1. Check with your teacher. 2. a. We walked along the bank of the river. 　 b. Father understood the semaphore signals. 　 c. Birds were calling all through the woods. 3. a. After a while we came to a bend in the river. 　 b. Suddenly a black train emerged from a tunnel. 　 c. Our next stop was the platelayer's cottage.
14	66	1. Shortest sentence: 3 words. 　 Sentences in paragraphs 1–5: 46. 　 Sentences in paragraphs 6–12: 63. 2. *Paragraph 5* 　 Number of sentences: 8. 　 Total words: 161. 　 Average sentence length: 20. 3. *Paragraph 6* 　 Number of sentences: 7. 　 Total words: 58. 　 Average sentence length: 8. 　 The sentence length changes dramatically in each half of the story. Overall average sentence length in the first half of the story (21) is twice that of the second half (11).

Answers for Project 2 Exercises

These are suggested answers. In some cases your wording may differ slightly. If in doubt, check with your teacher.

Exercise title	Page	Answers
1. Colloquial style:	67	a. We were cruising just a little above the clouds (or similar phrase). b. There were no more than five empty seats (or similar phrase). c. The flight was uneventful, I recall, until we crossed the coast (or similar phrase). d. I remember very well the noise was so loud it seemed it would deafen me (or similar phrase).
2. Description and contrast:	67	a. roared, howled b. winked, pulsed c. smelled, stank d. cool, icy
3. Sentence length – increasing the pace:	68	a. The wing tilted up abruptly. The aeroplane banked left. Everyone on board was suddenly silent. b. It began to get dark. The clouds became grey as we climbed. Mother and I looked out at the coming night. c. We passed low over a light tower. The beacon pulsed in the dark below. Red light soaked the cabin.
4. Sentence length – slowing the pace:	68	a. A river meandered far below like a silver thread, running through a patchwork of fields. b. There was a rustle of movement as passengers unclipped their seatbelts and stretched, reaching for earphones and magazines. c. Outside were clouds that slid calmly by as we hovered far above.

Project 3: Write a personal essay

Introduction

IN THIS SECTION:
- Preview the task

An essay is a short discussion that explores a topic in some depth and presents a viewpoint or opinion to the reader. Essays can be written on any topic that takes the writer's interest, from cats to climate change. Whatever the subject, the goal of an essay is the same: to explore the topic from a number of angles in order to improve the reader's understanding of it.

Essays can be written in many styles and may take a variety of approaches – personal, factual, scientific, philosophical, and more. This project focuses on the *personal essay*. In a personal essay, the writer presents his or her own thoughts honestly and clearly, often drawing on personal experience or popular wisdom. Personal essays often have a friendly, intimate tone that makes them emotionally persuasive to the reader.

The word "essay" comes from the French verb *essayer*, which means "to attempt". Each essay is an "attempt" on a topic, an effort to say something wise or clever about it. If the writer is successful, the essay will entertain and enlighten the reader. Modern writers famous for their essays include George Orwell, James Baldwin, Susan Sontag, Clive James and Zadie Smith.

Learning to write a good essay is a challenge. It may require you to draw on many other skills, including epigram, explanation, argument and storytelling. It can also be good preparation for other kinds of writing, such as feature articles and reviews.

Goal: Write a personal essay that explores a familiar topic from a range of different angles.

Skills you will learn in this project:
- shaping your essay *topic*
- stating your *thesis* using *values* and *argument*
- organising your essay using *divisions*
- presenting your topic from *different angles*
- controlling *diction* and *style*
- using special tricks of persuasion: *exaggeration, quotation, rhetorical questions*

Special terms: *exordium, apodixis, apomnemonysis, hyperbole, erotesis*

Step 1: The model

IN THIS SECTION:
- Read an example
- Explore its features and usage

For this project you will copy a personal essay by the famous French writer, Michel de Montaigne (1533-1592). Montaigne is considered the inventor of the essay. He was at various times a lawyer, diplomat, Member of Parliament, and city mayor. He was also a sceptical thinker, who liked to challenge the ideas of his time.

When he retired from public service, Montaigne began writing short accounts of his thoughts and experiences. He called these short pieces *essays*. Two volumes of his work, containing 94 essays, were published in 1580. A third volume, containing 13 more, was published in 1588. Although written over 400 years ago, the essays still seem quite modern in thought and style.

Montaigne died in 1592 of quinsy, an inflammation of the tonsils.

Before reading

In this essay, Montaigne shares with us his thoughts about liars and the practice of lying. He explores the topic from a number of angles. He discusses the connection between lying and memory, different kinds of lying, and gives an example of a liar who was caught out.

Read the essay carefully and note *the different ideas about lying* that are discussed.

Words to know:

faculty – a sense or ability (e.g. intelligence, memory, compassion)

lamentable – regrettable, unfortunate

maundering – rambling, moving slowly or dreamily

obstinacy – stubbornness, inflexibility

prompter – a person who reminds stage actors of their lines when they forget them

Plato – a famous Greek philosopher, who lived around 400 BC

Pythagoreans – followers of the mathematician and philosopher, Pythagoras

St Augustine – an early Christian philosopher and scholar, who lived around 400 AD

On Liars

1 There is no man so unsuited for the task of speaking about memory as I am, for I find scarcely a trace of it in myself, and I do not believe there is another man in the world so hideously lacking in it. All my other faculties are poor and ordinary, but in this I think I am most rare and singular, and deserve to gain name and fame thereby.

5 Plato was right in calling memory a great and powerful goddess. In my country, when they want to say that a man has no sense, they say that he has no memory; and when I complain of the shortcomings of my own, people correct me and refuse to believe me, as if I were accusing myself of being a fool. They can see no difference between memory and intellect. This makes me look much worse off. But they wrong me, for experience shows that, on the
10 contrary, excellent memories are often coupled with feeble judgements. They also wrong me when they find fault with my affections instead of my memory. "He has forgotten this request or that promise," they say. "He doesn't remember his friends. He did not remember to do this, to say that, or to keep quiet about the other, for my sake." Certainly I am prone enough to forgetfulness, but as for neglecting, out of indifference, a service which a friend
15 has asked of me, that I do not do. Let them be content with my misfortune and not turn an involuntary defect into a wilful one. For I am nothing if I am not a good friend.

But I find some benefits in my poor memory. First, I have derived from this evil my principal argument against a worse evil, which might have taken root in me: the evil of ambition. For lack of memory is an intolerable defect in anyone who takes on the burden
20 of the world's affairs. Secondly, nature has generously strengthened other faculties in me in proportion as my memory has grown weaker. I might easily have let my intelligence and judgement follow languidly in other men's footsteps, if other people's ideas and opinions had ever been present with me by favour of my memory. And, my speech is consequently briefer, for the storehouse of the memory is generally better stocked with material than
25 that of the invention.

If my memory had been good, I should have deafened all my friends with my chatter, since any subject that excites me warms and extends my speech. This would have been lamentable, as I have learned in the case of some of my intimate friends. As their memory gives them a complete and first-hand view of their subject, so they look back further and
30 burden their narrative with useless details. If the story is a good one, they smother its virtues; if it is not, you curse either their fortunate powers of memory or their unfortunate lack of judgement. There is no better way of proving a horse's strength than by pulling him up short and sharp. Even among men who keep to the point, I find some who would like to break off but cannot. While they are searching for a place at which to stop, they go
35 maundering and trailing on like a man who is losing strength. Particularly dangerous are old men who retain the memory of past events, but do not remember how often they have repeated them.

I find some consolation, also, in the fact that I have a short memory for the insults I have received. Like the Persian King, Darius, I would need a prompter to remind me. Wishing not to forget the insult he had suffered from the Athenians, the King made one of his pages come and repeat three times in his ear, each time he sat down to table: "Sire, remember the Athenians." It consoles me, too, that the places I revisit and the books I re-read always smile upon me with the freshness of novelty.

Not without reason is it said that no one who has a bad memory should set out to be a liar. I know quite well that grammarians make a distinction between telling an untruth and lying. They say that to tell an untruth is to say something that is false, but that we suppose to be true; while to tell a lie is to say the opposite of what one knows. The Latin word *mentiri,* from which our French word for lying derives, means to go against one's conscience. It is of those conscious liars that I am speaking.

Now liars either invent the whole thing, or they disguise and alter an actual fact. If they disguise and alter, it is hard for them not to get mixed up when they refer to the same story again and again. The real facts having been the first to lodge in the memory and impress themselves upon it, they will spring into the mind and dislodge the false versions, which cannot have as firm a foothold. The circumstances, as they were first learned, will always rush back into the thoughts, driving out the memory of the false or modified details that have been added. If liars make a complete invention, they apparently have much less reason to be afraid of tripping up, in as much as there is no contrary impression to clash with their fiction. But even a complete invention readily escapes from the memory unless it is a very reliable one.

I have often had amusing proof of this fact, at the expense of those who change their stories to suit the circumstances or to please the great men to whom they are speaking. As circumstances change, their language has also to change from time to time; and so they call the same thing grey one moment and yellow the next, say one thing to one man, and another to another. Then, if these listeners happen to bring all this contrary information together as a common booty, what becomes of all their fine art? For what memory could be strong enough to retain all the different shapes they have invented for the same subject?

Lying is indeed an accursed vice. We are men, and we have relations with one another only by speech. If we recognised the horror and gravity of an untruth, we should more justifiably punish it with fire than any other crime. I commonly find people taking the most ill-advised pains to correct their children for their harmless faults, and worrying them about heedless acts which leave no trace and have no consequences. Lying – and to a lesser degree obstinacy – are, in my opinion, the only faults whose birth and progress we should consistently oppose. They grow with a child's growth, and once the tongue has got the knack of lying, it is difficult to imagine how impossible it is to correct it. So it happens that we find some otherwise excellent men subject to this fault and enslaved by it. I have a decent lad as my tailor, whom I have never heard to utter a single truth, even when it would have been to his advantage.

If, like the truth, falsehood had only one face, we would be better off, for we should then take the opposite of what a liar said to be the truth. But the opposite of a truth has a hundred thousand shapes and a limitless field. The Pythagoreans regard good as certain and finite, and evil as boundless and uncertain. There are a thousand ways of missing the
80 bull's eye, only one of hitting it. I am not sure that I could induce myself to tell a brazen and deliberate lie even to protect myself from the most obvious and extreme danger. St Augustine says that we are better off in the company of a dog we know than in that of a man whose language we do not understand. Therefore those of different nations do not regard one another as men, and how much less friendly is false speech than silence!

85 On this point, King Francis the First once boasted of having run rings around an ambassador sent to him by the Duke of Milan. The Duke had cut off the head of a gentleman named Merveille, on a false charge of murder, the trial having been hurried through and the sentence carried out at night. Now this gentleman had been acting for the King, with the Duke's knowledge; but the ambassador came with a long, falsified account of the whole
90 affair. He advanced several plausible justifications of the deed, carefully prepared for the purpose. He pleaded that his master, the Duke, had taken Merveille for a private citizen who had come to Milan on his own business. He denied all knowledge that Merveille was a member of the King's household.

King Francis pressed objections and questions upon the ambassador, attacking him from
95 all sides and cornering him at last on the point of the execution, carried out at night and apparently in secret. To which the poor embarrassed man replied, as if to put an honest face on the matter, that out of respect for His Majesty, the Duke would have been sorry to let the execution take place in daylight. You can guess how quickly he was caught out in this clumsy self-contradiction, made in the presence of such a nose as King Francis had.
100 The ambassador's property was confiscated, and he barely escaped with his life.

Michel de Montaigne
Translated by J.M.Cohen
(abridged and adapted)

After reading

Montaigne explores the topic of liars through personal reflection, rather than through scientific study or logical analysis. Nevertheless, his essay is carefully organised. There are five clear sections, called *divisions,* which explore the topic from different angles. The essay also uses many *persuasive techniques* to convey his ideas and get the audience on his side – including some subtle humour.

Activity 1

1. Montaigne's essay has five main *divisions*. Below are descriptions for each division. Put the descriptions in the correct order (number them 1 to 5), and say where each section starts.

Description	Order		Line
a. The importance of memory		begins at line	
b. An example of a liar		begins at line	
c. Memory and lying		begins at line	
d. The nature of lying		begins at line	
e. Introductory declaration		begins at line	

2. Montaigne's discussion of lying contains many interesting ideas and statements. Find where he makes each of the points below, and number them in the correct sequence. (Use numbers 1-8.)

   a.   My memory is so bad I should be famous for it.   ☐

   b.   Telling an untruth is not the same as lying.   ☐

   c.   People who lie to please others will be found out.   ☐

   d.   Lying is the worst of human vices.   ☐

   e.   Many lies can take the place of one truth.   ☐

   f.   People with good memories often don't know when to shut up. ☐

   g.   Memory and intelligence are not the same thing.   ☐

   h.   A man with a bad memory cannot be a good liar.   ☐

3. What conclusions can be drawn from Montaigne's essay? Tick the options his essay supports.

   a.   It is better to have a poor memory than a good one.   ☐

   b.   It is better to say nothing than to tell a lie.   ☐

   c.   Honest people are more likely to be forgetful.   ☐

   d.   People who speak a foreign language cannot be trusted.   ☐

   e.   All lying is morally wrong.   ☐

   Discuss your choices with members of your group or class. Point to the sentences in the essay that support your decisions.

What's the use?

Essays are often written in response to current events. A natural disaster might prompt people to think about issues such as *chance, courage* or *charity*. The death of a famous figure might raise issues of *loss* and *hope*. Essay writers pick up on events like these, and take the opportunity to explore them in more depth. The essayist's job is to think carefully about the topic and share his or her observations with readers.

You should consider using the personal essay approach when you want to *explore some aspect of common experience* and *share your thoughts with a wider audience*. You can also use essay writing as a way of clarifying your own thoughts on a topic, in a diary or journal.

Essays can be found in newspapers, journals, and magazines. Many online blogs are personal essays by another name. Successful bloggers can now earn big incomes from their writing.

Activity 2

1. Essays are often written in response to a current event. Here are three events that could trigger someone to write an essay on liars. Add two more events to the list.

    a. a politician breaks an election promise
    b. a public official is found to have lied on his job application
    c. a foreign diplomat gives a false account of his government's actions
    d. ....
    e. ....

2. Here are some fictional current events. For each one, suggest two relevant topics that could be explored in an essay. (*Suggestions:* fame, mistrust, greed, hypocrisy, jealousy, ambition, faith)

Event	Topic 1	Topic 2
a. Famous couple sells first pictures of their baby to a magazine for $1 million.		
b. Prize-winning scientist takes credit for a co-worker's research, to steal funding.		
c. Study shows modern teenagers drink only as much as their parents did, but they get more criticism.		

Now that you have explored some features of essays and their uses, you are ready to look more closely at how an essay is assembled.

Step 2: Ideas and design

IN THIS SECTION:
- Learn to organise your ideas
- Learn to make a plan
- Write a first draft

Before you can write an essay like Montaigne's, you need to study how it is constructed. We will start our analysis by looking at the ideas and the design or arrangement of the material.

Ideas: topic and development

The first task of an essay writer is to choose a topic. Personal essays often have *general* topics, even if they are triggered by specific events.

Compare these different statements about liars.

Specific: Senator Smith was caught lying because he gave completely different stories to different groups in his electorate.

General: People who tell lies in an attempt to please others must have good memories if they do not want to be caught out.

The first statement refers to a specific person, while the second treats lying as a general feature of human behaviour. The first approach is a subject for a journalist, while the second is a topic for an essayist.

Montaigne's essay is of the second type – it is about liars *in general.*

Choosing a topic
The following four points should be considered when choosing a topic.

1. *Commonality – Is it part of common experience?* The best topics are often part of the common experience of people, or of a particular readership. People like to read about topics on which they already hold a view. Montaigne's essay on liars is a good example.

2. *Subjectivity – Is it a matter of opinion?* The topic should be something you can have an opinion on, or make judgments about. For example: you can have an opinion on which animals make the best pets, but not on the correct height for a satellite to orbit. One is a matter of opinion, the other a matter of mathematics.

3. *Accessibility – Can it be understood by everyone?* The topic should be one you can discuss in the language of ordinary people, given sufficient thought and effort. It should not require scientific or specialised knowledge that your readers will not have.

4. *Scope – Is it the right "size"?* You should be able to say something sensible about the topic in a short spac e. Some topics might too big to discuss in a short essay (e.g. the fate of the universe). Other topics might be too small (e.g. the flavour of cornflakes).

Activity 3

1. Which of the following topics would be best suited to the *personal essay* approach? On the basis of the criteria above decide whether each is *Suitable* or *Unsuitable*. Tick your choices.

Topics	S	U
a. the importance of friendship		
b. classifying the types of rhyme in early English poetry		
c. the rights and wrongs of illegally downloading music		
d. your pet dog/cat/guinea pig		
e. the meaning of life		
f. the lure of fashion		
g. the types of subatomic particles		
h. the quality of television programs		

For those topics you have labelled Unsuitable, say which "rule" influenced your decision.

2. The title for an essay should signal the topic clearly. Montaigne gave his essay a simple two-word title: "On Liars". Which of the following titles would you choose for an essay on *the rights and wrongs of illegally downloading music?* Pick one, or write your own.

a. On music   c. On piracy   e. On ....

b. On theft   d. On ownership   f. On ....

Create two-word titles for other "suitable" topics you selected above.

a. On ....   b. On ....   c. On ....

Development

Once you have framed your topic, your next task is to say something about it. This is called *development.* There are different *forms* of development. Some essays are developed by logic and argument, and they arrive at very specific conclusions. Others are developed by sheer volume of ideas, and may not arrive at a single viewpoint.

Montaigne's essay, "On Liars", uses a form of development called *accumulation.* He explores the topic from a number of angles, adding many observations and ideas as the essay progresses. He relies on gathering a lot of material together, rather than following a single argument.

A good starting point is to list your own thoughts on the topic. These first impressions will help you identify your own opinions.

Activity 4

1. Imagine that you are writing an essay on the topic of *friendship.* Make a list of *any thoughts* you have on the topic – even if they seem obvious or silly. Below are some suggested starting points that you might agree or disagree with. Add your own thoughts to the list.

    Everyone needs friends.
    The quality of friends is more important than the quantity.

2. Here are some questions that could be considered in an essay on friendship. Use the questions to suggest more ideas for your list above.

    What is a friend?
    Do friendships change over time?
    How should we treat our friends?
    What can we expect from friends?
    Are there different types of friends?
    Are there examples of famous friendships we can follow?

Research: sources and strategies

Having recorded your personal thoughts, the next step in developing your ideas is to *explore the topic from different angles.* That means doing some basic research. An essay writer needs to use outside knowledge, even when taking a personal approach. Useful resources for this research could include books of quotations, dictionaries, encyclopaedias and web sites.

Montaigne has used at least six different *sources and strategies* to build his discussion of liars. They include the following.

1. *Personal experience:* This is anything that has happened to the writer personally, or which he or she has seen first-hand.

2. *Authority:* This includes statements by famous people, experts on the subject, or other persuasive sources, such as a quotation from an encyclopaedia. Experienced writers often have a store of familiar quotations that they can use. (Quoting from authorities in this way is called *apomnemonysis.*)

3. *Definition:* This includes information about the meaning of words, their origins, or clarification of how a term is being used. Definitions can help focus an argument.

4. *Analysis:* This means breaking down a topic into its parts, and naming, labelling, classifying or explaining them. It is a useful way to clarify ideas.

5. *Maxim:* This includes popular sayings, commonly accepted principles, and truisms. Maxims are often traditional sayings among a group of people. (Quoting a maxim in order to prove a point is called *apodixis.*)

6. *Exemplum:* This is a specific example that illustrates the general topic.

Activity 5

1. These examples show the sources and strategies Montaigne used. Classify each one as personal experience (PE), authority (Au), definition (D), analysis (An), maxim (M) or example (E).

a. There is no better way of proving a horse's strength than by pulling him up short and sharp.	
b. I have a decent lad as my tailor, whom I have never heard to utter a single truth, even when it would have been to his advantage.	
c. King Francis the First once boasted of having run rings around an ambassador sent to him by the Duke of Milan.	
d. Liars either invent the whole thing, or they disguise and alter an actual fact.	
e. The Latin word *mentiri* means to go against one's conscience.	
f. St Augustine says that we are better off in the company of a dog we know than in that of a man whose language we do not understand.	

Look through the essay and see you if you can find one other example of each source or strategy. Share your findings with your group or class.

2. Below is a list of ideas and statements that could be used to develop an essay on friendship. Select *at least one* item in each category that would be useful in a discussion of friendship. Tick your choices; then record them in your note book. Add other ideas of your own.

Personal experience (Personal knowledge)	
A good experience of friendship	☐
A bad experience of friendship	☐
Other personal knowledge:	

Authority (Quotations)	
"Friendship often ends in love, but love in friendship never." *Charles Colton*	☐
"The best friend is the man who in wishing me well wishes it for my sake." *Aristotle*	☐
"A true friend stabs you in the front." *Oscar Wilde*	☐
"What is a friend? One soul dwelling in two bodies." *Aristotle*	☐
"Love is only chatter; friends are all that matter." *Gelett Burgess*	☐
Other quotations:	

Definition (Word meanings)	
The word "friend" comes from an ancient Germanic word meaning "to love".	☐
The word "friend" has the same origin as the word "free", meaning "to free" a person.	☐
The word "friend" is among the oldest words in our language, dating back over 5,000 years.	☐
Other definitions:	

Analysis (Logical study)	
There are two kinds of friends: true friends and false friends.	☐
Among children there two kinds of friends: best friends, and everybody else.	
Each of us has many types of friends: close and distant, past and present, boy and girl.	☐
Other analyses:	

Maxim (Popular sayings or rules)	
"True friends are like diamonds, precious and rare; false friends are like grains of sand, you find them everywhere."	☐
"A friend in need is a friend indeed."	☐
Other sayings:	

Exemplum (Specific example)	
Some famous friendships from television and film: Mulder and Scully (*The X Files*), Joey and Chandler, (*Friends*), Jerry and Elaine (*Seinfeld*).	☐
Other specific examples:	

Thesis: the key idea

After listing your own thoughts and doing some research, you should have enough ideas to begin your essay. You may also have found that the research has added to, or sharpened, your thinking. The final step in shaping your topic is to condense your thought into a key idea that sums up your opinion or viewpoint. This key idea is called the *thesis*. A good thesis can generally be expressed in one or two short statements.

Montaigne's view of liars could be summed up by these two statements:

> *Lying is a vice.*

> *A liar will always be caught out because true memories are stronger than false ones.*

The first statement is a *value* statement. It states whether the thing is good or bad, desirable or undesirable, and so on. The second statement is an *argument*. It draws a logical connection between ideas, showing cause and effect (signalled by the use of the word, "because").

Activity 6

1. Try to sum up your thesis on friendship using *two* statements: a *value statement* and an *argument*. Below are some suggestions to help guide you. Write your statements below them.

    a. Value statement (good or bad)

        e.g.   Friends are important/unimportant?
               Friends are the most/least/one important thing in life?

        Friends are: ....

    b. Argument (connection or cause)

        e.g.   We need friends because ....
               Quality is better than quantity because ....

        Your argument: ....

Writing a thesis: three rules

1. Form a clear opinion on the topic.

2. Write a value-statement that presents your opinion, e.g. *Lying is a vice.*

3. Summarise your argument using "because", e.g. *Liars will be caught because true memories are stronger than false ones.*

Design: arranging the ideas

Once you have done your research and defined your thesis, you need to arrange the material in the best order. Your essay will need a number of clear *divisions* or sections. Without a clear structure, the essay will be a jumble of ideas.

Montaigne's essay structure

Montaigne has structured his essay using firstly, a brief introduction (or *exordium)* followed by four more divisions in which his essay is developed. He has used those sources and strategies that he feels will best support his argument. The structure of his essay can be diagrammed as follows.

1. *Introduction:* The writer makes an amusing personal confession, or *declaration*, that catches the reader's attention. **I have the worst memory in the world!**	

2. *Personal experience:* The writer reflects on and discusses the value of memory, and how his poor memory has shaped his experiences.
 	
    People misjudge me because they confuse memory with intelligence.
 	
    My poor memory has benefits: it protects me from ambition; it stops me from relying on other people's ideas; it prevents me from boring my friends; it helps me forget insults.	

3. *Logical analysis:* The writer connects memory to lying; he divides liars into types, and gives definitions.
 	
    Lying means saying the opposite of what one knows.
 	
    Liars must therefore have good memories, because they must remember the stories they have made up.
 	
    But a good memory will catch them out, because their true memories will always come back to bite them.	

4. *Statement of values:* The writer states his opinion of liars.
 	
    Lying is an accursed vice.
 	
    We are better in the company of dogs than of people whose speech we cannot trust.	

5. *Exemplum:* The writer gives an example that illustrates his point.
 	
    King Francis caught a liar in the act.
 	
    The ambassador from Milan contradicted himself because his true memories betrayed him under questioning.	

Activity 7

1. Go back to Montaigne's essay beginning on page 78 and label the main divisions with the following headings. Then record the line number where each division begins.

Divisions	Numbers
1. Introduction	
2. Personal experience	
3. Logical analysis	
4. Statement of values	
5. Exemplum	

2. You can explore the design of a text by counting some of its features. Use the tables below to record some features of Montaigne's essay. More complete tables can be found on pages 147–8.

    a. Look firstly at the *divisions* used in Montaigne's essay.

Divisions	Numbers
Number of main *divisions* or sections	
Number of sentences in longest division	
Number of sentences in shortest division	
Average number of sentences per division (total number of sentences divided by the number of divisions)	

    b. Montaigne uses a number of techniques in order to *develop* his argument convincingly and logically. Tick those that he uses in the table below.

Methods of development	Used
Accumulation of detail/statement	
Examples or instances (giving examples to prove a point)	
Logical argument or proof	
Storytelling (using anecdotes to make or emphasise a point)	
Antithesis or contradiction (taking the opposing side, or showing a contrast)	
Authority (quoting other sources, such as famous people or experts)	
Maxims (quoting popular sayings)	

c. Now look at the ways in which Montaigne manages the *transitions* from one division to the next in his essay. Tick those used on the table below.

Transitions	Used
Assertion (a direct statement that advances the argument)	
Repetition of a word/phrase (e.g. Key words from previous part used to start next.)	
Linking words/phrases (e.g. Conjunctions: "However..."; numbering: "Thirdly...")	
Announcement (e.g. "We now turn to the matter of..."; "Let us consider...")	
Logical chains (e.g. If this, then that ...)	

3. What can you conclude from the information you have gathered?

Agree   Disagree

a. Montaigne devotes more space to personal experiences than values. ☐   ☐

b. Montaigne devotes more space to values than analysis. ☐   ☐

c. Montaigne uses one main technique of development. ☐   ☐

d. Montaigne uses announcement more than assertion, for his transitions. ☐   ☐

Planning a personal essay

Now that you have studied how to select your topic, and develop and arrange your material, you are ready to plan a personal essay. For your first attempt you will write an essay on the topic of friendship.

Activity 8

1. Use the template on the next page, "Plan for a personal essay – on friendship", to help you develop your own essay plan. The suggestions on the plan will help you to record your ideas *in note form*, using material from the activities you have completed above.

Plan for a personal essay – on friendship

Ideas

    Topic: Friendship

Thesis:	
Values:	....
	....
Argument:	....
	....
Materials:	Gather your notes on personal experience, authority, definition, analysis, maxim, and example.

Design

Introductory declaration:	Make an amusing personal confession to interest the reader. (*Suggestion:* comment on the kind of friend you are.)
Personal experience:	Discuss your experience of friendship; quote authorities. (*Suggestion:* discuss how your qualities as a friend affect your relationships; find a suitable quote that supports your experience.)
Logical analysis:	Set out your main arguments using definitions and analysis. (*Suggestion:* discuss the nature of friendship, types of friends; give a definition.)
Statement of values:	State your opinions; quote a relevant maxim. (*Suggestion:* state your "values" thesis; find sayings that support your values.)
Exemplum:	Give an example of a famous friendship that illustrates your thesis. (*Suggestion:* write about a real or fictional friendship that has influenced you.)

(*Note:* you can experiment with placing the divisions in a different order, to suit your topic.)

2. Once you have made your plan, go on and write the first draft of your essay. Do your best to develop your main ideas by building on the materials in your plan. Do not worry if your draft is not yet very polished.

> When you have written your draft, put it to one side. You will return to it as you work through the following section on style.

Copying or dictation

Study closely the first paragraph of Montaigne's essay on page 78. Pay attention to these things:

1. The length and wording of the sentences

2. The punctuation

3. The spelling (especially the spelling of unfamiliar words)

Copy the paragraph into your notebook, checking against the original as you go. Make sure you capture the wording and punctuation exactly. Alternatively, write out the paragraph as your teacher reads it aloud. When you are done, discuss any features of the writing that have come to your attention.

Step 3: Style

IN THIS SECTION:
- Learn the writer's techniques
- Learn about diction, sentence style and special features
- Improve your draft in stages

Now that you have learned to plan an essay you are ready to learn some techniques of style that will make your essay more readable and persuasive. In this section you will briefly explore three aspects of style: *diction, personal style,* and special *features of persuasion.*

Diction

The term *diction* refers to the words that are used in the writing. The words you use in an essay can have a powerful effect on the reader, so you must learn to choose them carefully. Two features you should consider when choosing your words are *connotation* and *complexity*.

Connotation

In making decisions about what words to use, you will need to consider the shades of meaning, or connotations, that accompany particular words. Look at the following terms, all of which have the same basic meaning.

   liar, dissembler, fabricator, fibber, perjurer, deceiver, pretender

These are all words for describing a person who does not tell the truth. But they have different shades of meaning. Some seem forgiving, while others seem to accuse or blame. We can arrange them in order from the most gentle ("fibber") to the most harsh ("liar"). Montaigne's decision to use the strongest and most direct of these terms in his essay creates an impression that he is being honest and direct with the reader. The essay would create a different impression if the wording was changed.

Activity 9

1. Compare these versions of Montaigne's thesis. The first is the original, the others alternative wordings. Which do you think has the strongest intensity? Which the least?

Lying is an accursed vice.	☐
Deceitfulness is a bad character flaw.	☐
Dissembling is an evil habit.	☐
Pretending is a loathsome defect.	☐

2. In the first draft of your essay, you will have used the word "friend" many times. The following are some possible alternatives. Can you add more to the list?

    comrade, buddy, soulmate, pal, acquaintance, ally, chum, crony, partner, cohort

3. The following statements all express the same basic idea about friendship. Mix and match the words from the different versions to create two more phrases.

    a. A true friend is rare jewel.

    b. A real mate is an uncommon prize.

    c. A genuine soulmate is a singular find.

    d. A bona fide chum is a scarce treasure.

    e. ....

    f. ....

    What different shades of meaning are there in these versions?

Complexity

The complexity of a word is shaped by features such as its length, its number of syllables, and its language of origin. Compare the words "eat" and "consume". They mean the same thing, but one seems simpler and more direct than the other. "Eat" is short, it has one syllable, and it comes from the Anglo-Saxon language. "Consume" is longer, it has two syllables, and it comes from Latin. English has many pairs of words like eat and consume. For example:

work	– labour		worsen	– exacerbate
meal	– repast		hobby	– recreation
stay	– sojourn		skull	– cranium

As a rule, short, simple words will make your writing seem direct, casual, earthy. Long, complex words will make your writing seem educated, sophisticated, scientific. But too many short words can seem simplistic or trite; and too many long words can seem pompous and distant. It is important to balance the diction of your writing with other features of style.

Montaigne often uses complex Latin-based terms and wordy phrases, which makes his writing seem sophisticated. However, he balances this tendency with other phrases that are more direct and casual. For example:

Complex: I am most rare and singular, and deserve to gain name and fame thereby.

Simple: I am nothing if I am not a good friend.

Activity 10

1. A good way to analyse diction is to count the different types of words in a passage. Use this table to identify and record some features of Montaigne's diction in paragraph 3 (beginning with the sentence, "But I find...." on page 78).

Types of words	Essay	Draft
Number of abstract nouns (e.g. love, hate, good, evil, benefit, ambition)		
Number of concrete nouns (e.g. desk, rock, plate, bread, hand, nose)		
Number of single syllable words (e.g. eat, work, food)		
Number of multi-syllable words (e.g. consume, labour, nourishment)		

Your findings should show that Montaigne's diction in this paragraph is highly abstract and contains a high proportion of multi-syllable words.

2. Do the same analysis on a passage of similar length in your draft essay. Compare your use of abstract nouns and multi-syllable words to Montaigne's.

3. The following phrases and sentences are *simpler* versions of Montaigne's writing. Replace the underlined words with more *complex* alternatives. You can choose your own, or find the originals in Montaigne's essay.

   a. My other <u>senses</u> are poor and ordinary...

   b. As for neglecting, out of <u>carelessness</u>, a service asked of me...

   c. I would not follow <u>lazily</u> in other men's footsteps...

   d. To deafen my friends with my chatter would have been <u>sad</u>...

4. The following are more *complex* versions of Montaigne's phrasing. Replace the underlined words with simpler versions. Choose your own, or find the originals in Montaigne's essay.

   a. If my memory had been <u>prodigious</u>, I should have deafened all my friends...

   b. This makes me look <u>much inferior</u>...

   c. People <u>reproach</u> me and refuse to believe me...

   d. It is hard for them not to get <u>befuddled</u>...

   For each of the above, decide if you prefer the simpler version or more complex one. Judge if the more complex word is really an improvement, and if it suits the style and purposes.

Vocabulary

Your ability to make good word choices will be influenced in part by your vocabulary – the number of words you know. The larger your vocabulary, the more choices you will have available to you. The average person is sometimes said to have a working knowledge of about 10,000 words, but experienced writers may have vocabularies much greater than this. Shakespeare is reported to have had a vocabulary of nearly 30,000 – but then, he made up a lot of his own words!

Activity 11

1. Here are two thesis statements that might be included in an essay on friendship.

   Value: Friends are essential.

   Argument: We need friends because life is too complex to survive alone.

   Here are the same statements re-worded; firstly, two reworded *value* statements and then their *arguments*. How many other variations can you produce, without changing the core meaning?

   Values: a.   Allies cannot be dispensed with.

                  b.   We cannot do without companions.

                  c.   ....

                  d   ....

   Argument: a.   We need close companions, for the world is too multifaceted to go solo.

                  b.   Our lives being complex, we must have comrades to assist us.

                  c.   ....

                  d.   ....

2. You might be surprised to learn that it is possible to produce *hundreds* of variations on these sentences. Ancient teachers of rhetoric used this activity to teach their students flexibility, and to extend their vocabulary. As an exercise, you might like to see just how many variations you can produce, using only the *values* statement, "Friends are essential", above.

> Go back to your draft essay and experiment with your diction. Review the balance of simple and complex words, and try rephrasing some of your key statements. Be sure that you make changes to get the *meaning* you want; if more complex words don't *improve* the writing, don't use them.

Personal style

Montaigne discusses complex ideas in his essay, and his writing *is* sometimes long-winded and rambling. However, he manages to create a sense of intimacy with the reader, as if speaking on equal terms with a friend. He achieves this impression of personal contact in two ways: through frequent use of personal pronouns, and through the use of popular sayings and idiomatic phrases.

Personal pronouns

Montaigne writes his essay in the *first person*, making frequent use of the personal pronouns "I" and "we". He also occasionally uses the *second person* "you" as if to include the reader in a conversation. These are features of a casual, personal style.

Examples: "*I* have a decent lad as my tailor..."

             "*We* have relationship with one another only through speech..."

             "*You* curse their fortunate powers of memory..."

Popular sayings and idiomatic phrases

People who share a similar way of life also share common ways of saying things. They share popular phrases that are traditional to the group, such as mottoes and maxims. For example: "A fool and his money are soon parted." They also share idiomatic sayings. These are sayings that do not actually make literal sense. For example: "To give someone the hairy eyeball" means to be angry or to give a look of warning. This kind of saying is confusing for outsiders – they can work out the meaning of the saying about "a fool and his money" from the individual words, even if they have never heard the phrase before. But they cannot work out the "hairy eyeball" phrase, because it does not make literal sense. Why would a person give someone an eyeball? Why would the eyeball be hairy? Using idiomatic phrases with someone is a way of signalling closeness and friendship.

These examples also show the difference between a popular and an idiomatic saying.

Popular: There is only one way to hit the bullseye, and a thousand ways to miss.

Idiomatic: The King ran rings around the ambassador.

Personal style: two rules

1. Write in the first person ("I") and occasionally address the reader as "you".

2. Use some of your favourite sayings and idiomatic phrases, *when appropriate.*

Activity 12

1. Go back to Montaigne's essay and find more examples of personal pronouns that are used to create a sense of closeness with the reader. Underline four examples and note their line numbers.

2. Search the essay for other popular sayings or idiomatic phrases. You should be able to find at least one of each.

> Go back to your draft and review your use of personal pronouns and popular sayings. Check that you have used "I" and "we" to create a sense of intimacy with your readers.

Special persuasive devices

In addition to the techniques of style and arrangement explored above, Montaigne uses two traditional tricks designed to get a reader on side: *hyperbole* and *erotesis*.

Hyperbole

Hyperbole is exaggeration. The word comes from an ancient Greek phrase that means "to throw too far". Thus, hyperbole is any claim that goes beyond the facts. Montaigne begins his essay with the claim that he has the worst memory of any man in the world:

> "I do not believe there is another man in the world so hideously lacking in [memory]. All my other faculties are poor and ordinary, but in this I think I am most rare and singular, and deserve to gain name and fame thereby."

This is an exaggeration used for humorous effect. Starting with an amusing claim makes Montaigne seem down-to-earth, and helps put the reader at ease.

Erotesis

An *erotesis* is a question that is asked in such a way that everyone knows the expected answer. Such questions are also called *rhetorical questions*. In an essay, the writer asks such a question not because he wants an answer (the reader cannot give him one) but as a strategy to make the reader "fill in" the expected answer in his or her head. Montaigne uses *erotesis* in paragraph 8, when he discusses the strain on a liar's memory from telling too many lies to too many people:

> "... if these listeners happen to bring all this contrary information together as a common booty, what becomes of all their fine art? For what memory could be strong enough to retain all the different shapes they have invented for the same subject?"

The *purpose of the question is to invite the reader to agree* with Montaigne's view that liars will always be caught out by failures of memory.

Activity 13

1. Which of the following phrases count as *hyperbole?* (Tick your choices.)

    a. I am surely the most neglectful friend in the history of the world. ☐

    b. Every friendship, like every snowflake, is unique. ☐

    c. Let's face it, a good friend is more important than oxygen. ☐

    d. Friends, like food and shelter, are one of life's necessities. ☐

2. Which of the questions below are examples of *erotesis* or are "rhetorical"? (Tick your choices.)

    a. Which of us doesn't need a friend from time to time? ☐

    b. What time is the next bus due? ☐

    c. Is the word, "friend", Anglo-Saxon or Latin in origin? ☐

    d. Who would not be shocked by a bus that arrived on time? ☐

Go back to your draft and check whether there are opportunities for you to use hyperbole and erotesis in ways that will contribute to your argument and your readers' enjoyment.

You have now finished revising your draft essay.

Go to Step 4 on page 101 if you want more practice in diction and special features of persuasion.

OR

Go straight to Step 5 on page 102 to write your final copy.

Step 4: Exercises (optional)

IN THIS SECTION:
- Practise your new skills

The exercises that follow will give you more practice in diction and features of persuasion. Answers are on page 107. When you are ready, go on to Step 5.

1. *Diction – vocabulary:* Exercise your vocabulary by writing down five different words for:

   a. love, b. loyal, c. enemy and d. hate.

2. *Diction – judgement:* Rate the following phrases as earthy, subtle, direct, indirect, or pompous.

   a. You don't rat on your mates.
   b. One doesn't dob in a friend.
   c. You don't surrender those who love you.
   d. One doesn't inform on one's compadres.
   e. A man with his head in a noose doesn't offer up the chair he stands on; so it is with friends.

3. *Diction – complexity:* Replace the underlined words with more complex alternatives. You can choose your own, or find the originals in Montaigne's essay.

   a. I find some <u>comfort</u> in the fact that I have a short memory for insults...
   b. They go <u>wandering</u> and trailing on...
   c. It <u>cheers</u> me that the places I re-visit smile upon me...

4. *Diction – simplicity:* Replace the underlined words with simpler, more direct alternatives. You can choose your own, or find the originals in Montaigne's essay.

   a. I have a <u>respectable</u> lad as my tailor...
   b. The ambassador came with a long, <u>confabulated</u> account...
   c. The King boasted of having <u>comprehensively defeated</u> an ambassador...

5. *Special features of persuasion – hyperbole:* Which of the following phrases count as hyperbole?

   a. It was a friendship to outlast the pyramids.
   b. She had friendships so brief they could only be measured with a stopwatch.
   c. Their friendship was so strong, it reached beyond the borders that kept them apart.

6. *Special features of persuasion – erotesis:* Which questions are examples of erotesis or are "rhetorical"?

   a. Who would not prefer a friend to an enemy?
   b. Who said, "Hell is other people"?
   c. Where do people find their friends nowadays?

Step 5: The final copy

IN THIS SECTION:
- Put it all together
- Write the final copy
- Hand it in

Now you are ready to write the final version of your essay. Use the skills you have learned to create an essay that matches the design and style of Montaigne's essay.

On page 103 is a checklist you or your teacher can use to assess your work.

Summary: Formula for a personal essay

Purpose
To clarify your thinking on a topic; to share your ideas with others.

Ideas
- Choose a topic.
- Consider *generality, commonality, subjectivity, accessibility, scope.*
- Current events may suggest a topic.
- Develop your topic:
  - Note down your thoughts.
  - Research the topic.
  - Make notes under the headings authority, definition, analysis, maxim, exemplum.
  - Write your thesis, using a value statement and an argument statement.

Design
- Organise your material into divisions:
  - 1. Introductory declaration; 2. Personal experience and reflection; 3. Logical analysis; 4. Values statement; 5. Exemplum.

Style
- Use personal pronouns to create trust and intimacy.
- Balance the complexity of your diction:
  - Use some complex vocabulary to create authority and sophistication.
  - Use simpler language to create directness.
- Experiment with different ways of wording your key phrases.
- Consider using techniques of *hyperbole* (exaggeration) and *erotesis* (rhetorical questions) to influence your reader.

Assessment checklist: Project 3

Score your work as follows: 2 points for each *Yes;* 1 point for *Partly*; 0 points for each *No.*
Add the scores for a mark out of 22.

Project 3: Write a personal essay	
Ideas	**Tick the box**
Is it a suitable topic? (Consider generality, commonality, subjectivity, accessibility, scope.)	No ☐ Partly ☐ Yes ☐
Does the main thesis include clear values and arguments?	No ☐ Partly ☐ Yes ☐
Design	
Does the essay have clear divisions? (e.g. introduction, personal reflection, logical analysis, values, exemplum.)	No ☐ Partly ☐ Yes ☐
Are the ideas developed using a range of strategies? (e.g. personal experience, authority, definition, analysis, maxim, example.)	No ☐ Partly ☐ Yes ☐
Are the divisions well balanced with effective connections and transitions?	No ☐ Partly ☐ Yes ☐
Style	
Are personal pronouns ("I", "we") used to establish intimacy and trust?	No ☐ Partly ☐ Yes ☐
Is the vocabulary well balanced?	No ☐ Partly ☐ Yes ☐
Are Latin-based words used to create authority?	No ☐ Partly ☐ Yes ☐
Are Anglo-Saxon words used for directness?	No ☐ Partly ☐ Yes ☐
Are techniques such as *hyperbole* (exaggeration) or *erotesis* (rhetorical questions) used for persuasive effect?	No ☐ Partly ☐ Yes ☐
Spelling and punctuation	
Is the spelling correct? Is punctuation and general usage correct?	No ☐ Partly ☐ Yes ☐
Comment:	
Date:	Score:

Going further

IN THIS SECTION:
■ Get ideas for further writing

1. Michel de Montaigne published over 100 essays on a wide range of topics. In addition to his essay, "On Liars", he wrote on the following topics: laziness, friendship, fear, good intentions, the custom of clothing, educating children, loneliness, sleep and age.

   Choose one of these topics and write your own essay, following the formula you have learned in this project. Then find Montaigne's original and compare your essay with his.

2. Montaigne's works have been translated by a number of different writers. Some of these translations differ greatly from one another. Find two versions of the essay "On Liars" by different translators, and compare the two pieces. Write a report on your findings, under the following headings.

   a. Details of the two versions (e.g. translator, date)

   b. General discussion of the differences (look at word choice, sentences, tone)

   c. A detailed comparison of one section

   d. Evaluation (say which you think is better)

3. Collect news reports from a daily paper or online news service, and note down essay topics suggested by the reports. In your class or group, select a topic to write on, and compare the resulting essays. Mount a display or website containing the original news report and the essay commentaries.

4. Start a diary, journal or web log in which you try to write one brief essay each week, for four weeks, on a topic suggested by current events.

5. Collect examples of essays appearing in weekly magazines or blogs. Find an author whose work you like, and give a presentation to your class or group about his or her work. You could report on:

   a. The publication where you found the essays

   b. Some of the topics covered

   c. The writer's stye and techniques

   d. Your personal evaluation of the work

Quiz: Project 3

1. State three biographical facts about Michel de Montaigne.

....

2. State the origin and meaning of the term *essay*.

....

3. Give the names of three famous essayists, other than Montaigne.

....

4. Explain each of the following forms of development: *authority, maxim, exemplum*.

....

5. Name the two components of a thesis.

....

6. State the five main divisions in Montaigne's essay.

....

7. What is the difference between connotation and complexity in word choice? Give an example of each.

....

....

8. What is an idiomatic phrase? Give an example.

....

9. What are *hyperbole* and *erotesis?*

....

10. State the meaning of *maundering* and *obstinacy.*

....

Answers for Project 3 Activities

These are suggested answers. In some cases your wording may differ slightly. If in doubt, check with your teacher.

Activity	Page	Answers
1	81	1. The correct order is 1e.(Introduction, line 1); 2a. (Importance of memory, line 5, "Plato was right..."); 3c. (Memory and lying, line 44, "Not without reason..."); 4d. (Nature of lying, line 66, "Lying is indeed an accursed..."); 5b. (An example of a liar, line 85, "On this point...") 2. The sequence is 1a, 2g, 3f, 4h, 5b, 6c , 7d, 8e. 3. This is a topic for discussion. All of the statements are supported to some degree.
2	82	1. This is a self checking task. 2. Suggestions: a. fame & greed; b. ambition & jealousy; c. hypocrisy & mistrust.
3	84	1. Unsuitable: b. (Rule 1); d. (Rule 4); e. (Rule 4); g. (Rule 1). 2. This is a self-checking task.
4	85	1. & 2. These are self-checking tasks.
5	86–7	1. a. maxim, b. personal experience, c. example, d. analysis, e. definition, f. authority. 2. This is a self-checking task.
6	88	1. This is a self-checking task.
7	90–1	1. Discuss with your teacher. 2. a. Divisions: 5; Sentences in longest division: 29; in shortest division: 2; Average 14. 2. b. All of the methods are used *except* antithesis. 2. c. The main forms of transition are *assertion* and *repetition of key words*. 3. a. is true.
8	91–3	These are self-checking tasks. Discuss with your teacher.
9	94–5	1, 2. & 3. Discuss with your teacher.
10	96	1. There are more than 20 abstract nouns (some repeated); there are no concrete nouns. There are 50 multi-syllable words out of 125. Most of the single syllable words are minor (articles, prepositions etc.) 2. This is a self-checking task. 3. a. faculties, b. indifference, c. languidly, d. lamentable. 4. a. good, b. worse off, c. correct, d. confused.
11	97	1. & 2. These are self-checking tasks. Discuss with your teacher.
12	99	1. Check with your teacher. 2. Other phrases include "hitting the bullseye" and "such a nose as King Francis had". *Footnote:* Montaigne's essay has been translated from the original French. The style is therefore a combination of Montaigne's original work and decisions made by the translator, J.M. Cohen. For convenience, however, the writer is referred to as "Montaigne".
13	100	1. a. and c. are most clearly hyperbolic. 2. a. and d. are most clearly rhetorical.

Answers for Project 3 Exercises

These are suggested answers. In some cases your wording may differ slightly. If in doubt, check with your teacher.

Exercise title	Page	Answers
1. Diction – vocabulary:	101	a. affection, adoration, worship, devotion, passion, ardour... b. true, steadfast, faithful, devoted, trusty... c. foe, adversary, rival, combatant, antagonist... d. enmity, odium, revulsion, disgust, contempt...
2. Diction – judgement:	101	a. earthy, b. direct, c. subtle, d. pompous, e. indirect.
3. Diction – complexity:	101	a. consolation, b. maundering, c. consoles.
4. Diction – simplicity:	101	a. decent, b. falsified, c. run rings around.
5. Features – hyperbole:	101	a. and b. are hyperbolic.
6. Features – erotesis:	101	a. is an example of erotesis, or is a rhetorical question; the others seem to require an answer that is not entirely self-evident.

Project 4: Write a speech

Introduction

IN THIS SECTION:
- Preview the task

A speech is a formal talk delivered to a live audience. The formal speech is one of the most ancient forms of public address. Before newspapers, or radio, or television, or the internet, leaders and rulers used speeches to inform and influence people. The same is true today. Most important social and cultural events are accompanied by speeches.

There are three common types of speech: ceremonial, expository and persuasive. *Ceremonial* speeches are used to mark an occasion, such as an anniversary, a wedding, or a funeral. *Expository* speeches are used to present information or state a case on some issue. *Persuasive* speeches are used to change people's minds or urge them to take some kind of action. Most speeches combine, to some degree, all three elements of ceremony, exposition and persuasion.

The goal of every speech is to influence the audience. A speech can affect how people *feel*, how they *think*, or how they *act*. Ancient orators developed special techniques for achieving these things. They learned how to stir emotions, how to appeal to reason, and how to urge people to action, using nothing more than words, voice and gesture. Many of their techniques are still used. In this project you will learn these skills by preparing your own persuasive speech.

Goal: Write a speech encouraging support for an action or policy, giving attention to elements of ceremony, exposition and persuasion.

Skills you will learn in this project:
- balancing the elements of a speech: *ceremony, exposition, persuasion*
- building an argument using *assertion* and *proof*
- organising your speech through *traditional divisions*
- persuading an audience through *emotion, reason* and *ethics*
- persuading an audience through *apostrophe* and *exhortation*
- signposting your speech with *pointing, linking* and *number phrases*
- using special features of *style*

Special terms: *antistrophe, anaphora, auxesis, parallelism*

Step 1: The model

IN THIS SECTION:
- Read an example
- Explore its features and usage

For this project you will copy a famous speech by an Australian Prime Minister. In February 2008, the Australian Parliament issued a formal apology to the nation's Indigenous people for government policies that had separated children from their families. The speech was written and delivered by Kevin Rudd, who was then the Prime Minister. Rudd had worked as a diplomat, bureaucrat and consultant before becoming leader of the Australian Labor Party in December 2006. He was elected the nation's 26th Prime Minister in December 2007.

Before reading

On the next page is an abridged transcript of the speech. The apology was controversial, and Australians held strong opinions for and against it. Kevin Rudd's speech therefore had to unite people on the issue and present arguments in favour of the apology.

The speech had to consider a range of different audiences. Many groups of people were present in Parliament on the day: the Speaker (chair) and Members of the House; Indigenous elders and community representatives; and members of the public. The speech was also broadcast live to the nation. Although Rudd sometimes speaks directly to the Speaker, or to others who were present or watching on television, his speech is directed to the nation as a whole; and he speaks on behalf of the government and the white community. This makes the relationships between speaker and audience quite complex.

To make his meaning clear to all groups, Rudd develops his topic in stages and in a variety of ways. In the speech you will find: background information about the reasons for the apology; a statement of the purpose of the speech; a brief story about a real person, Nana Fejo; facts and figures about past events; statements of sorrow and regret; an outline of future intentions.

Read the speech carefully, paying attention to the techniques used to influence people's thoughts, feelings and actions.

Words to know:

    reconcile – to restore friendly relations between groups

    rancorous – full of bitterness and bad feeling

    partisan – one-sided, supporting one party

Apology to Australia's Indigenous Peoples

1 Mr Speaker, there comes a time in the history of nations when their peoples must become fully reconciled to their past if they are to go forward with confidence to embrace their future. Our nation, Australia, has reached such a time. That is why the parliament is today here assembled: to deal with this unfinished business of the nation, to remove a great stain
5 from the nation's soul and, in a true spirit of reconciliation, to open a new chapter in the history of this great land, Australia.

Last year I made a commitment to the Australian people that if we formed the next government of the Commonwealth we would in parliament say sorry to the stolen generations. Today I honour that commitment. I said we would do so early in the life of the new parliament.
10 Again, today I honour that commitment by doing so at the commencement of this the 42nd parliament of the Commonwealth. Because the time has come, well and truly come, for all peoples of our great country, for all citizens of our great Commonwealth, for all Australians – those who are Indigenous and those who are not — to come together to reconcile and together build a new future for our nation.

15 Some have asked, "Why apologise?" Let me begin to answer by telling the parliament just a little of one person's story – an elegant, eloquent and wonderful woman in her 80s, full of life, full of funny stories, despite what has happened in her life's journey, a woman who has travelled a long way to be with us today, a member of the stolen generation who shared some of her story with me when I called around to see her just a few days ago.

20 Nanna Nungala Fejo, as she prefers to be called, was born in the late 1920s. She remembers her earliest childhood days living with her family and her community in a bush camp just outside Tennant Creek. She remembers the love and the warmth and the kinship of those days long ago, including traditional dancing around the camp fire at night. She loved the dancing...

25 But then, sometime around 1932, when she was about four, she remembers the coming of the welfare men. Her family had feared that day and had dug holes in the creek bank where the children could run and hide. What they had not expected was that the white welfare men did not come alone. They brought a truck, two white men and an Aboriginal stockman on horseback cracking his stockwhip. The kids were found; they ran for their mothers,
30 screaming, but they could not get away. They were herded and piled onto the back of the truck. Tears flowing, her mum tried clinging to the sides of the truck as her children were taken away to the Bungalow in Alice, all in the name of protection. Nanna Fejo never saw her mum again.

I asked Nanna Fejo what she would have me say today about her story. She thought for a few moments then said that what I should say today was that all mothers are important. And she added: "Families – keeping them together is very important. It's a good thing that you are surrounded by love and that love is passed down the generations. That's what gives you happiness." As I left, later on, Nanna Fejo took one of my staff aside, wanting to make sure that I was not too hard on the Aboriginal stockman who had hunted those kids down all those years ago. The stockman had found her again decades later, this time himself to say, "Sorry". And remarkably, extraordinarily, she had forgiven him.

Nanna Fejo's is just one story. There are thousands, tens of thousands of them: stories of forced separation of Aboriginal and Torres Strait Islander children from their mums and dads over the better part of a century... These stories cry out to be heard; they cry out for an apology. Instead, from the nation's parliament there has been a stony, stubborn and deafening silence for more than a decade; a view that somehow we, the parliament, should suspend our most basic instincts of what is right and what is wrong; a view that, instead, we should look for any pretext to push this great wrong to one side, to leave it languishing with the historians, the academics and the cultural warriors, as if the stolen generations are little more than an interesting sociological phenomenon.

But the stolen generations are not intellectual curiosities. They are human beings, human beings who have been damaged deeply by the decisions of parliaments and governments. But, as of today, the time for denial, the time for delay, has at last come to an end. The nation is demanding of its political leadership to take us forward. Decency, human decency, universal human decency, demands that the nation now step forward to right an historical wrong. That is what we are doing in this place today.

But should there still be doubts as to why we must now act, let the parliament reflect for a moment on the following facts: that, between 1910 and 1970, between 10 and 30 per cent of Indigenous children were forcibly taken from their mothers and fathers; that, as a result, up to 50,000 children were forcibly taken from their families; that this was the product of the deliberate, calculated policies of the state as reflected in the explicit powers given to them under statute; that this policy was taken to such extremes by some in administrative authority that the forced extractions of children of so-called "mixed lineage" were seen as part of a broader policy of dealing with "the problem of the Aboriginal population"...

These are uncomfortable things to be brought out into the light. They are not pleasant. They are profoundly disturbing. But we must acknowledge these facts if we are to deal once and for all with the argument that the policy of generic forced separation was somehow well motivated, justified by its historical context and, as a result, unworthy of any apology today.

Then we come to the argument of intergenerational responsibility, also used by some to
70   argue against giving an apology today. But let us remember the fact that the forced removal
of Aboriginal children was happening as late as the early 1970s.

The 1970s is not exactly a point in remote antiquity. There are still serving members of this
parliament who were first elected to this place in the early 1970s. It is well within the adult
memory span of many of us. The uncomfortable truth for us all is that the parliaments of the
75   nation, individually and collectively, enacted statutes and delegated authority under those
statutes that made the forced removal of children on racial grounds fully lawful.

There is a further reason for an apology as well: it is that reconciliation is in fact an
expression of a core value of our nation – and that value is a fair go for all. There is a deep
and abiding belief in the Australian community that, for the stolen generations, there was
80   no fair go at all. There is a pretty basic Aussie belief that says that it is time to put right this
most outrageous of wrongs.

It is for these reasons, quite apart from concerns of fundamental human decency, that
the governments and parliaments of this nation must make this apology – because, put
simply, the laws that our parliaments enacted made the stolen generations possible. We,
85   the parliaments of the nation, are ultimately responsible, not those who gave effect to our
laws. And the problem lay with the laws themselves. As has been said of settler societies
elsewhere, we are the bearers of many blessings from our ancestors; therefore we must also
be the bearer of their burdens as well. Therefore, for our nation, the course of action is clear:
that is, to deal now with what has become one of the darkest chapters in Australia's history.

90   In doing so, we are doing more than contending with the facts, the evidence and the often
rancorous public debate. In doing so, we are also wrestling with our own soul. This is
not, as some would argue, a black-armband view of history; it is just the truth: the cold,
confronting, uncomfortable truth – facing it, dealing with it, moving on from it. Until we
fully confront that truth, there will always be a shadow hanging over us and our future as
95   a fully united and fully reconciled people. It is time to reconcile. It is time to recognise the
injustices of the past. It is time to say sorry. It is time to move forward together.

To the stolen generations, I say the following: as Prime Minister of Australia, I am sorry. On
behalf of the government of Australia, I am sorry. On behalf of the parliament of Australia,
I am sorry. I offer you this apology without qualification. We apologise for the hurt, the pain
100   and suffering that we, the parliament, have caused you by the laws that previous parliaments
have enacted. We apologise for the indignity, the degradation and the humiliation these
laws embodied. We offer this apology to the mothers, the fathers, the brothers, the sisters,
the families and the communities whose lives were ripped apart by the actions of successive
governments under successive parliaments.

105 I say to honourable members here present: imagine if this had happened to us. Imagine the crippling effect. Imagine how hard it would be to forgive. My proposal is this: if the apology we extend today is accepted in the spirit of reconciliation, in which it is offered, we can today resolve together that there be a new beginning for Australia. And it is to such a new beginning that I believe the nation is now calling us.

110 Australians are a passionate lot. We are also a very practical lot. For us, symbolism is important but, unless the great symbolism of reconciliation is accompanied by an even greater substance, it is little more than a clanging gong. It is not sentiment that makes history; it is our actions that make history... The truth is: a business-as-usual approach towards Indigenous Australians is not working. Most old approaches are not working. We

115 need a new beginning – a new beginning which contains real measures of policy success or policy failure...

Let us resolve today to begin with the little children – a fitting place to start on this day of apology for the stolen generations. Let us resolve over the next five years to have every Indigenous four-year-old in a remote Aboriginal community enrolled in and attending a

120 proper early childhood education centre or opportunity and engaged in proper preliteracy and prenumeracy programs. Let us resolve to build new educational opportunities for these little ones, year by year, step by step, following the completion of their crucial preschool year. Let us resolve to use this systematic approach to build future educational opportunities for Indigenous children to provide proper primary and preventive health care for the

125 same children, to begin the task of rolling back the obscenity that we find today in infant mortality rates in remote Indigenous communities – up to four times higher than in other communities.

None of this will be easy. Most of it will be hard – very hard. But none of it is impossible, and all of it is achievable with clear goals, clear thinking, and by placing an absolute

130 premium on respect, cooperation and mutual responsibility as the guiding principles of this new partnership on closing the gap.

The mood of the nation is for reconciliation now, between Indigenous and non-Indigenous Australians. The mood of the nation on Indigenous policy and politics is now very simple. The nation is calling on us, the politicians, to move beyond our infantile bickering, our

135 point-scoring and our mindlessly partisan politics and to elevate this one core area of national responsibility to a rare position beyond the partisan divide.

Mr Speaker, today the parliament has come together to right a great wrong. We have come together to deal with the past so that we might fully embrace the future. We have had sufficient audacity of faith to advance a pathway to that future, with arms extended
140 rather than with fists still clenched. So let us seize the day... Let us turn this page together: Indigenous and non-Indigenous Australians, government and opposition, Commonwealth and state, and write this new chapter in our nation's story together. First Australians, First Fleeters, and those who first took the oath of allegiance just a few weeks ago. Let's grasp this opportunity to craft a new future for this great land: Australia. I commend the motion
145 to the House.

Prime Minister Kevin Rudd (2007–2010)
(abridged)

After reading

Kevin Rudd's speech is a carefully crafted document. The apology was a controversial issue, and the Prime Minister had to be sure that his speech did not create further division in the community. The speech had to create a sense of unity and agreement among many different groups of people. The choice of language and the arrangement of the material reflect this aim. The speech moves back and forth between grand concepts and simple stories, between elevated rhetoric and everyday words, between talking about the victims and talking to them.

Activity 1

1. The speech has a number of distinct sections. Find each of the following sections in the speech, and number them in the order in which they appear.

Sections	Order
a. a brief outline of events leading up to the speech	
b. a statement of purpose	
c. a conclusion that says change will be difficult	
d. a brief story about a real person	
e. a statement of facts and figures	
f. an introduction that states the importance of the apology	
g. a brief outline of future actions	

2. Rudd gives *three* reasons why an apology to Indigenous people is needed. Find the three reasons in the speech, and number them. Then tick the correct options below.

    An apology to Indigenous people is needed because:

    a. real people have been hurt. ☐
    b. the hurt was deliberate policy, not accident. ☐
    c. Australian values are at stake. ☐
    d. the law requires it. ☐
    e. other nations expect it. ☐

3. Find examples of the following in the speech and label them. Then record the line numbers of where the statements occur.

Statements	Line numbers
a. a statement addressed directly to the members of parliament	
b. a statement addressed directly to the victims of separation	
c. a statement addressed to all the people of Australia	

4. The language and style of the speech varies a great deal. Find examples of the following and label them. Record the line numbers of where the examples occur.

Features	Line numbers
a. grand language that signals the importance of the occasion	
b. simple, direct language that makes the PM sound like an "ordinary bloke"	
c. phrases that call on people to join together	
d. phrases that create emphasis through repetition	

5. Which of the following statements best sums up the overall argument of the speech?

    a. An apology is needed to heal the nation. ☐
    b. An apology is needed to deliver justice. ☐
    c. An apology is needed to avoid lawsuits. ☐

What's the use?

Speeches are an important and powerful form of communication. Even in a world of electronic media, the live speech remains significant. Politicians in particular understand that a good speech makes the presenter look powerful and statesmanlike. (It also shows a degree of courage. A live audience can answer back and make life difficult for the speaker.) In our private lives, too, we employ the art of speechmaking to mark important events. Graduations, weddings, funerals, and other occasions can be made more significant through good speeches.

Most important speeches are not delivered off the cuff; they are carefully scripted beforehand. Senior politicians and public figures often employ speechwriters, whose job is to create speeches that are stylish, memorable and persuasive. These writers know how to win over an audience by arranging material in the best order and using the right language.

Speeches are not all the same. The kind of speech needed to announce a war is very different from that needed to announce a new discovery – or to give an apology. Kevin Rudd's speech is an example of a talk that is partly *persuasive* and partly *ceremonial*. Its goal is not only to convince people that the government's policy is correct, but also to create a sense of occasion and national unity. You should use this kind of speech when you want to *gather people together in agreement on a controversial issue.*

Activity 2

1. Few people are ever required to present a speech to an entire nation, but most of us will have to give speeches of some kind at various times in our lives. Here are four speech scenarios. Rank them from highly ceremonial (1) to minimally ceremonial (4) based on the degree of ceremony and persuasion required.

   a. *A valedictory or graduation speech.* The aim is to encourage the graduating class to become good and active citizens.

   b. *A speech to a government inquiry* considering new laws on organ donation. The aim is to support the passing of new laws making donation automatic.

   c. *A speech to a campus rally* organised in support of students expelled for downloading music illegally. The aim is to get people to sign a petition calling for the decision to be reversed.

   d. *A wedding speech.* The aim is to welcome the guests and praise the bride and groom.

2. Describe one other speech that would require *high* levels of ceremony and persuasiveness. Share your suggestion with others in your group or class.

Now that you have explored some features of Kevin Rudd's speech, you are ready to learn how to write your own.

Step 2: Ideas and design

IN THIS SECTION:
- Learn to organise your ideas
- Learn to make a plan
- Write a first draft

Before you can learn to write a speech like Kevin Rudd's, you need to study how the speech is constructed. We will start our analysis by looking at the ideas, and their design or arrangement.

Ideas: arguments and persuasion

Like a persuasive essay, Kevin Rudd's speech presents an argument to the audience. It aims to convince people that giving an apology is the right thing to do. The argument for making an apology is developed in two parts – called *assertion* and *proof.*

Argument: the assertion

An *assertion* is a statement of belief or action. The main assertion is the key point of the speech. It is the idea that everything else in the speech is designed to support.

The key assertion in Kevin Rudd's speech can be stated like this:

> The government must apologise to Indigenous people because it has done them wrong, and because the nation must be healed.

The assertion includes an element of *action* (i.e. giving an apology) and an element of *explanation* (i.e. the apology is needed because...). These are the key ideas of the speech. In preparing your own persuasive speeches, you must have a clear idea of your key assertion.

Activity 3

1. Imagine a speech designed to support a government policy making organ donation automatic. Which statement gives the clearest argument? (Look for *action* and *explanation*.)

   a. We believe that it is in the best interests of the sick to allow the automatic donation of organs. ☐

   b. We must support automatic organ donation because the needs of the sick must outweigh the rights of the dead. ☐

   c. We must place the rights of sick people, who could benefit from healthy organs, above the rights of the dead. ☐

2. Write assertions on the topics below, including *action* and *explanation* in your statements. (*Hint:* make a statement implying an action followed by an explanation – action is needed *because*...)

    a. A statement supporting more funding for solar power research. The main argument is that solar power is cleaner than power from fossil fuels.

    b. A statement attacking plans to raise the driving age. The main argument is that young people as a group should not suffer because of the bad driving of a few.

3. The main assertion of Kevin Rudd's speech can be found in the second paragraph. Underline the action statement and the explanation. (*Hint:* They are not in the same sentence.)

Argument: the proof

The key assertion in any speech must be backed up with *proof*. In speechmaking, the "proof" is anything that will make the assertion more convincing. It might include facts and figures, but it might also include material that is purely emotional or purely traditional in appeal.

Kevin Rudd's speech contains three forms of proof.

1. *A human story – Nanna Fejo:* Kevin Rudd briefly tells the story of Nanna Fejo. Telling one person's story gives a human face to the issues and invites the audience to make a personal connection. The story can be about a real person, or it can be a fictional person who represents the experiences of many real people. The human story is a form of *exemplum* or example. Stories of this kind appeal mainly to the *emotions* of the audience.

2. *Facts and figures – 50,000 children:* Rudd's speech includes information about the number of children separated from their families (50,000) and the time span of the policy (1910–1970). Including figures is a way of informing the audience about the facts and conveying the scale of the problem. A speech should not contain too many facts and figures, because they can make for dull listening. But a few well-chosen numbers or dates can be effective. Factual information of this kind appeals to the *reasoning skills* of the audience.

3. *Values and principles – a "fair go":* Rudd states that the policy of forced separation conflicts with Australian values, such as the belief in a "fair go". This is a statement about national values and principles. By linking the apology to a value that Australians hold dear, Rudd suggests that rejecting the apology would be un-Australian. Values and principles can be presented in many forms: through popular sayings, quotations, or even through fables. Using values or principles to persuade people is called *apodixis*. These statements of value appeal to the audience's sense of character and *ethics*.

These three kinds of proof have been used by speakers through the ages. They appeal to basic forces that sway human action: emotion, reason and ethics. Ancient orators called these *pathos, logos* and *ethos*.

Activity 4

1. Find the three proofs in Kevin Rudd's speech and highlight each one. Label them using these titles: *human story* (emotion); *facts and figures* (reason); *values and principles* (ethics).

2. The following are proofs that could be used to support an argument in favour of organ donation. Classify each one as an appeal to *emotion, reason* or *ethics*.

    a. About 2,000 Australians receive organ transplants each year.

    b. Michael, a young music student in Sydney, is one of 1,800 people waiting for a life saving donation. He knows that with a kidney transplant his future prospects are grim.

    c. It is an Australian tradition to help your mates. Those on organ waiting lists need all the mates they can get.

    d. Only 200 Australians each year donate their organs. One donor can provide life-saving organs for 10 people.

    e. Bumper sticker: "Don't take your organs to heaven. Heaven knows we need them here."

Argument: persuasion

As well as offering proofs to support his argument, Kevin Rudd uses two other techniques to persuade his audience. These techniques work by engaging the audience, making them feel involved in the events and actions.

1. *Turning aside (apostrophe):* Toward the end of his speech, Rudd pauses to speak directly to the victims of family separation: "To the stolen generations, I say the following…" This technique of "turning aside" to speak to people, not all of whom are actually present, is called *apostrophe*. It is a way of drawing attention to a specific group of people and including them in the event. An *apostrophe* is often announced with an opening phrase such as, "To the victims, we say…" (*Note:* the punctuation mark that we call "apostrophe" has the same meaning: it marks the place where a missing letter has been "turned aside".)

2. *Calling together (exhortation):* After his *apostrophe*, Rudd turns back to the wider audience and calls upon them to join together and act as one: "I say to the honourable members here present: imagine if this had happened to us… Let us resolve today to begin…" Calling upon the audience to act together is called *exhortation*. It is a way of creating a sense of unity and purpose. An exhortation often contains the phrases, "Let us…" or "We shall…"

Activity 5

1. Find the *apostrophe* ("turning aside") and *exhortation* ("calling together") in Kevin Rudd's speech. Highlight and label them.

2. The following statements come from a speech about organ donation. Classify each one as either *apostrophe* (A) or *exhortation* (E).

Statements	A	E
a. To those on the waiting lists, and to their friends and families, we say: we are here to help.		
b. Let us all resolve to take action. Let us all resolve right here, right now, to give the gift of life.		
c. Michael, you cannot be with us today, but we say to you, we will not abandon you, mate.		
d. We shall no longer stand by while our fellow Australians suffer the agony of waiting. We shall act together to ensure a better future for all.		

3. Turn these statements into *apostrophe* or *exhortation* by using the appropriate phrases.

    a. A statement calling on the audience to vote for more support for crime victims.

    "Let us ...."

    b. A statement addressed to victims of crime telling them they will not be forgotten.

    "To .... we say ...."

Design

In ancient times, scholars recommended that every persuasive speech should have certain key stages or *divisions*. The divisions and their purposes were as follows.

Exordium: the *introduction* calling the audience together.

Narration: the brief *background* "story" that led to the speech.

Partition: the main *assertion* of the speech and outline of topics to be addressed.

Confirmation: the major *proofs* and reasons for accepting the assertion.

Refutation: the *opposing arguments* and reasons for rejecting them.

Peroration: the grand *conclusion,* ending in hope and unity.

Professional speech writers and scholars still use these divisions today. They may know them by different names and may change the order of the divisions or collapse some divisions together to suit their purposes. However, the divisions they use to sequence their ideas are still very similar to the ancient stages of a persuasive speech.

The divisions

Kevin Rudd's apology speech conforms very closely to the ancient formula. We can describe the divisions in his speech as follows.

1. *Introduction:* The introduction addresses the audience ("Mr Speaker...") and states the significance of the occasion ("There comes a time in the history of nations..."). The introduction to the speech reminds the audience why they have gathered.

2. *Assertion:* The assertion begins with a brief outline of events leading up to the speech ("Last year, I made a commitment..."). It ends with the main assertion ("the time has come...to reconcile together and build a new future").

3. *Proofs:* This is the longest section in the speech. Here the speaker outlines the argument and presents evidence in support of the assertion. The proofs are chosen to appeal to the audience's *emotions, reason* and *ethics.* In Kevin Rudd's speech, the key proofs are the human story, facts and figures, and values.

4. *Persuasion:* Following the proofs, Kevin Rudd uses *apostrophe* and *exhortation* to speak to different parts of his audience, both present and absent. ("To the stolen generations, I say...") He also outlines future actions that will flow from the apology. Speakers sometimes use this part of a speech to consider and reject opposing arguments.

5. *Conclusion:* In the conclusion of his speech, Kevin Rudd openly admits the difficulties that are ahead. He states that the changes will be hard, but he concludes by showing optimism and praising the country ("Let's grasp this opportunity...for this great land: Australia"). This kind of grand, uplifting conclusion is used to create a sense of unity and hope for the future. It also rounds off the speech by repeating ideas from the opening. (Rudd's final sentence repeats a key sentence from the introduction.)

We can diagram the arrangement of Kevin Rudd's speech like this.

1. *Introduction*	
Addresses the audience:	"Mr Speaker..."
Announces the occasion:	"There comes a time in the history of nations..."
2. *Assertion*	
Gives the background:	"Last year, I made a commitment..."
States the assertion:	"An apology is needed because..."
3. *Proofs*	
Presents a human story:	"Nanna Fejo"
Presents facts and figures:	"50,000 children"
Presents values and principles:	"A fair go for all"
4. *Persuasion*	
Speaks to specific groups, both present and absent:	"To the stolen generations, I say..."
Speaks to those present:	"I say to the honourable members here..."
5. *Conclusion*	
States the difficulties:	"None of this will be easy..."
Gives optimism and praise:	"... a new future for this great land: Australia."

Signposts

Without a written text to refer back to, it is easy for listeners to lose track of the ideas in a long or complex speech. Experienced speechwriters take care to include "verbal signposts" that help the audience keep track of what is being said. There are three common types:

1. Pointing phrases
2. Linking phrases
3. Numbering phrases

Pointing phrases

Most speeches address multiple listeners. Pointing phrases "point" to the particular section of the audience being addressed. This helps listeners follow the speech and also allows the speaker to direct specific appeals or arguments to particular members of the audience.

Here are two examples of pointing phrases in Kevin Rudd's speech.

"I say *to the honourable members* here..."
"*To the stolen generations,* I say..."

Linking phrases

Linking phrases are important aids to listener's understanding of a speech. They help connect one part of the speech to another, and make it easier to follow.

Here are some examples of common linking phrases:

Let me start by saying...

I will now turn to the issue of...

The points I have just made clearly show...

Let me turn now to the topic of...

To those who disagree I say...

Linking phrases either announce a topic or connect one topic to another.

Numbering phrases

The third common type of signposts are numbering phrases. They help listeners keep track of the points within each part of the speech. This is done by saying aloud how many points there are in each section.

Here are some common examples of numbering phrases:

There are *three good reasons* to support this action...

The *first point* I would like to make is...

The *second point* in my argument is...

This brings me to my *third and final point...*

These phrases are used to tell the audience *in advance* how many points the speaker will make, and to number the points as they are made during the speech. (Did you notice that *number phrases* have been used in this section about signposts?)

You should always include pointing phrases, linking phrases and number phrases in a speech, to make sure your audience does not get lost.

Activity 6

1. Find the divisions in the speech and label them recording the line number where they begin.

Description	begins at	Line
1. Introduction	begins at	
2. Assertion	begins at	
3. Proofs	begins at	
4. Persuasion	begins at	
5. Conclusion	begins at	

2. Kevin Rudd's speech contains a variety of *signpost phrases*. Find the following in the speech and decide whether each one is a pointing (P), linking (L) or numbering (N) phrase.

Signpost phrases	P	L	N
a. Let me begin to answer by telling one person's story...			
b. There is a further reason for an apology as well...			
c. It is for these reasons...			
d. To the stolen generations, I say...			
e. I say to honourable members here...			

3. The three main proofs in Kevin Rudd's speech have not been introduced using number phrases. Find the following sentences and re-write each one by inserting a number phrase.

   a. Let me begin by telling one person's story...
   b. Should there still be doubts as to why we must act, let the parliament reflect for a moment on the following facts...
   c. There is a further reason for an apology as well...

   Do you think numbering phrases would have made Kevin Rudd's apology speech easier to follow?

Planning a speech

Now that you have studied the ideas and design of Kevin Rudd's speech, you are ready to plan your own. For your first attempt, you will develop a speech on another controversial topic: *organ donation.*

About the topic

The Australian government is considering a change to the law, making organ donation automatic when a person dies. Imagine that you are the speechwriter for the Minister for Health or the opposition (shadow) Minister for Health. Write a speech, either for or against the proposal, for your boss to deliver at a public meeting on the issue. Your speech must be powerful and persuasive. It should convince voters to support one side of the debate.

Activity 7

1. On page 126 is a table summarising the cases for and against automatic donation. Choose *one* side of the argument, and familiarise yourself with the information and arguments in the table to plan your speech.

2. Now make a plan in *note form*. Use the headings and examples on the outline plan on the next page to help you organise your ideas.

Plan for a persuasive speech – on organ donation

Ideas

Issue:	Should we support automatic donation?
Assertion:	Make an action statement ("We should..."/ "We should not...") Give an explanation, i.e. briefly say why ("because...").
Developing your argument:	Use the information from the table to develop your argument.
Main proofs:	Write down three proofs that you will use.

Design

I. Introduction	
Address your audience:	Use polite, ceremonial phrases (e.g. "Ladies and gentlemen", "My fellow Australians", "Members of the Donor Society...").
Announce the occasion:	State the topic/purpose (e.g. "We are here today to support the many Australians with chronic diseases, whose only hope for a normal life..."). Stress the importance of the occasion (e.g. Our decision here today will affect many lives...).
2. Assertion	
Give the background:	Recount the events leading to the speech (e.g. "As you know, the government recently announced...").
State your assertion:	Action and explanation.
3. Proofs	
Present a human story:	(e.g. "Let me begin by telling you one person's story...")
Present facts and figures:	(e.g. "If anyone is still in doubt, let us consider the facts...")
Present values and principles:	(e.g. "As a final reason, let us consider the values of our nation...")
4. Persuasion	
Speak to those who are absent:	Make them feel included and cared for (e.g. "To those on the waiting lists, we say...").
Speak to those who are present:	Make them feel united in feeling and action (e.g. "To all of you who have gathered here today, I say..."; "Let us all agree to...").
5. Conclusion	
State the difficulties ahead:	(e.g. "The change will not be easy...")
End with optimism and praise:	(e.g. "We can and will succeed in..."; "We owe it to these people, our friends, and to this great country, Australia.")

Notes for a speech on the topic of organ donation

The issue
Should everyone be considered a donor after death, unless they have specifically opted *out;* or should no-one be considered a donor unless they have specifically opted *in?*

For automatic donation	Against automatic donation
Assertion	Assertion
Action: We must support automatic donation. *Explanation:* The living must have priority over the dead.	*Action:* We must reject automatic donation. *Explanation:* Silence does not equal consent.
Developing the argument	Developing the argument
Most people actually support donation. Donor rates are low only because people don't get around to filling in the donor card. Making donation automatic would solve the problem.	Many people do not support donation, for religious or other reasons. They may not have the time or language skills to register as non-donors. Their silence should not be taken as consent.
Main proofs	Main proofs
1. *Human story:* Michael, a promising young musician. Has kidney disease. Has been waiting two years for a transplant. His life is on hold until a suitable donor kidney is found. His whole family is affected. Why should he suffer? 2. *Facts, figures:* Australian population is 20 million. 1800 people are on waiting lists. Only 200 people donate each year, the lowest rate of donation in developed world. One donor can save 10 lives. 3. *Values:* Common sayings/principles – Look after your mates. A fair go for all. Australia is the "lucky country". [Choose one.]	1. *Human story:* Simone, a young teacher killed in an accident. Her organs were removed due to confusion over permission. Family and friends are devastated because her religion forbids donation. Could this become more common? 2. *Facts, figures:* Australian population is 20 million. 1800 people are on waiting lists; a small number of the population as a whole. The need for donation is rare, so a policy of automatic donation is excessive. 3. *Values:* Common sayings/principles – The needs and rights of the many outweigh the needs of the few. Prevention is better than cure. [Choose one.]
Apostrophe	Apostrophe
Turn aside to speak to those on the waiting lists. "To them, we say..."	Turn aside to speak to those who oppose donation on moral or religious grounds. "To them we say..."
Exhortation	Exhortation
Call upon the audience to act together. Useful phrases: "How would we feel if...?"; "Let us... "; "We shall..."	Call upon the audience to act together. Useful phrases: "How would we feel if...?"; "Let us... "; "We shall..."

3. Once you have made your plan, go on and write the first draft of your persuasive speech. Do your best to imitate the design and the writing style of the apology speech on pages 110–114. Do not worry if your draft is not yet very polished.

> When you have written your draft, put it to one side. You will return to it as you work through the following section on style.

Copying or dictation

Study closely the opening paragraph of Kevin Rudd's speech of apology on page 110. Pay attention to these things:

1. The length and wording of the sentences

2. The punctuation used

3. The spelling (especially the spelling of unfamiliar words)

Copy the lines into your notebook, checking against the original as you go. Make sure you capture the wording and punctuation exactly. Alternatively, write out the lines as your teacher reads them aloud. When you are done, discuss any features of the writing that have come to your attention.

Step 3: Style

IN THIS SECTION:
- Learn the writer's techniques
- Learn about diction, sentence patterns and special features
- Improve your draft in stages

Now that you understand the overall design of Kevin Rudd's speech, it is time to examine the style – that is, the way words and sentences are used. The activities that follow will help you learn about two important aspects of style: *diction* and *sentence patterns*.

Diction

The term *diction* refers to the words that are used in the speech. The choice and arrangement of words has a powerful effect on the audience, and is the speaker's most important technique for informing and persuading people. Kevin Rudd's speech contains an interesting mix of two styles of diction – the *grand* and the *common*.

Two styles

In an important speech, one of the speaker's tasks is to create an uplifting sense of *occasion*. This is done by using language that is "grand" and poetic. But the speech must also appeal to ordinary people, creating a sense of equality. This is done by using some language that is "common" and ordinary. We can see both styles at different points in Kevin Rudd's speech.

Look at these examples:

Grand: [T]here comes a time in the history of nations when their peoples must become fully reconciled to their past if they are to go forward with confidence to embrace their future. Our nation, Australia, has reached such a time. That is why the parliament is today here assembled: to deal with this unfinished business of the nation, to remove a great stain from the nation's soul and... open a new chapter in the history of this great land, Australia.

Common: There is a pretty basic Aussie belief that says that it is time... Australians are a passionate lot. We are also a very practical lot... The truth is, a business as usual approach towards Indigenous Australians is not working. Most old approaches are not working. We need a new beginning...

The *grand style* is used to create an impression of great seriousness. It makes the events surrounding the speech seem noble, historic, perhaps even heroic. The diction of the grand style includes *formal words* and *rarely used or poetic phrases,* such as "become fully reconciled," "stain on the nation's soul," and "this great land". It may also include traditional phrases such as "history's pages" and "the world stage". The grand style tends to be *wordy* (using many words to convey an idea).

The *common style* is used to show that the Prime Minister has not lost touch with ordinary people. It creates an impression that Australians are sensible, practical people who are not fooled by symbolism. The diction of the common style includes ordinary, everyday words and phrases such as "a passionate lot", "Aussie" and "business as usual". It may also include popular sayings, such as "a fair go". The common style tends to be *compact* (using few words to convey an idea).

Style and formality
To understand the difference between the two styles, we need to look closely at the concept of *formality* in diction. Look at this list of words:

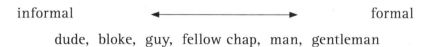

informal ←————————————→ formal

dude, bloke, guy, fellow chap, man, gentleman

They all mean basically the same thing, but not all of these choices would be appropriate on a given occasion. On occasions of great social importance, or when we wish to be serious and respectful, we would use "gentleman". It is the most formal choice. On more casual occasions, with friends and family, we might use "guy". It is an informal choice.

The English language gives us a lot of flexibility to choose words that match the formality of the occasion. The grand style used by Kevin Rudd contains many words and phrases from the more formal category – that is words that signal seriousness, respect, and importance.

Activity 8

1. Sort these lists of words in order from the *least formal* to the *most formal.*

    a. child, ankle biter, rugrat, minor, youngster, kid, brat, spawn, infant, toddler

    b. mob, group, people, community, crowd, lot, bunch

2. Sort these sentences into two lists: *grand* (formal) and *common* (informal).

Sentences		Grand	Common
a.	We need a fresh start.		
b.	We yearn for a new beginning.		
c.	Aussies are an optimistic mob.		
d.	Australians are an optimistic people.		
e.	We turn to the usual suspects.		
f.	We fix our attention upon history's scapegoats.		
g.	We must become fully reconciled to our history.		
h.	We must accept the past.		
i.	It is time to remove the great stain on our nation's soul.		
j.	It is time to put things right.		

3. Rewrite each of the following statements, changing the style as needed.

a. *Common:* Hi everyone. Thanks for having me here.

    Grand: ....

b. *Common:* Thanks for listening.

    Grand: ....

c. *Grand:* We have a proud tradition of benevolence to those in need.

    Common: ....

d. *Grand:* This gathering is a watershed in our recent history.

    Common: ....

e. *Grand:* The road ahead is long and hard, and our burden will be heavy.

    Common: ....

(*Suggested phrases:* track record; ladies and gentlemen; helping the needy; a turning point; the future; a tough road; kindness to others; grateful for your indulgence.)

4. Rewrite this paragraph to give it a *grander* style. Change the underlined sections so that they match the formality of the paragraph overall.

> Folks, it is really great to be here with you all at what I believe is a big event in the history of public health reform in Australia. I want to share with you lot my government's plan for fixing up an issue that is both a national crisis and a national disgrace. As we stand here today thousands of our Aussie citizens face an uncertain future. They are the innocent victims of trauma and chronic disease, and across this continent of ours, they are dying. They are dying not for want of cash, nor for want of doctors. They are dying not for want of a hospital bed or a bottle of potion. They are dying, I am sorry to say, for want of generosity. Our generosity.

(Possible words and phrases to choose from: my friends; ladies and gentlemen; fabulous; a great pleasure; a real hoot; historic moment; you today; tackling; addressing; Australian comrades; fellow Australians; great and prosperous land; wide brown land; vast country; finance; money; box of pills; vial of medicine.)

Read your final version aloud. Listen carefully for any phrases that seem out of place.

> Go back to your draft and examine your use of grand style and common style. Check that you have used a grand style in those places where you want to stress the *importance and seriousness* of the topic. Check that you have used a common style in at least one paragraph, to appeal to your audience as *an ordinary person*.

Ceremonial diction

Formal speeches are not only about making an argument; they are also *ceremonial occasions*. That means they must follow certain the rules of politeness and forms of ritual. The *diction* of your speech should take account of these rules and rituals.

People like to feel respected and included. You can show respect for the audience and encourage them to feel included in two main ways:

1. through the forms of *address* you choose

2. by using *inclusive language*.

Addressing the audience

It is a custom to begin your speech by addressing the audience directly. When you do this, you should use polite and respectful language. That means using correct titles for any dignitaries who may be attending.

The following are examples of polite address in different contexts.

Public speech:	Ladies and gentlemen...
Speech to a committee or board:	Mr Chairman, ladies and gentlemen...
Speech in parliament:	Mr Speaker, honourable members, ladies and gentlemen...
Speech at school:	Mr Skinner, parents and teachers, fellow students...

In the body of your speech you should continue to use these forms of address when you address the audience.

Inclusive language

Successful speakers use inclusive language to engage the audience and win them over. One way they do this is by using the personal pronouns "I", "you", and "we". In everyday conversation we often leave these words out. In a speech, we often emphasise them in order to build a relationship with the audience. For example:

Conversation:	Thanks for listening.
Formal speech:	I thank you for listening.

Inclusive language can be especially powerful when used in repeated phrases, such as: "*We say,* there must be change. *We say,* there *will* be change!"

Activity 9

Find examples in Kevin Rudd's speech on pages 110–114 of addressing the audience and inclusive language. Circle some examples and label them.

Check through your draft to make sure you have used polite forms of address when referring to the audience, and that you have used inclusive language to win the audience over to your side.

Sentence patterns

Two features stand out in the sentence patterns used by Kevin Rudd. The first is *length* and the second is *structure*.

Length

The length of sentences in Rudd's speech varies between those sections written in grand style and those in common style. Look at the following two examples.

Section A (grand style)

Mr Speaker, there comes a time in the history of nations when their peoples must become fully reconciled to their past if they are to go forward with confidence to embrace their future. Our nation, Australia, has reached such a time. That is why the parliament is today here assembled: to deal with this unfinished business of the nation, to remove a great stain from the nation's soul and, in a true spirit of reconciliation, to open a new chapter in the history of this great land, Australia.

Last year I made a commitment to the Australian people that if we formed the next government of the Commonwealth we would in parliament say sorry to the stolen generations. Today I honour that commitment. I said we would do so early in the life of the new parliament. Again, today I honour that commitment by doing so at the commencement of this the 42nd parliament of the Commonwealth. Because the time has come, well and truly come, for all peoples of our great country, for all citizens of our great Commonwealth, for all Australians — those who are Indigenous and those who are not – to come together to reconcile and together build a new future for our nation. (206 words)

Section B (common style)

I say to honourable members here present: imagine if this had happened to us. Imagine the crippling effect. Imagine how hard it would be to forgive. My proposal is this: if the apology we extend today is accepted in the spirit of reconciliation in which it is offered, we can today resolve together that there be a new beginning for Australia. And it is to such a new beginning that I believe the nation is now calling us.

Australians are a passionate lot. We are also a very practical lot. For us, symbolism is important but, unless the great symbolism of reconciliation is accompanied by an even greater substance, it is little more than a clanging gong. It is not sentiment that makes history; it is our actions that make history. The truth is: a business as usual approach towards Indigenous Australians is not working. Most old approaches are not working. We need a new beginning – a new beginning which contains real measures of policy success or policy failure. (169 words)

Activity 10

1. Consider the length of sentences in Section A (grand style) and Section B (common style), as shown in the table below.

Features	Number
Number of words in Section A	206
Number of words in Section B	169
Total number of sentences in Section A	8
Total number of sentences in Section B	12
Length of longest sentence in Section A	49
Length of longest sentence in Section B	35
Length of shortest sentence in Section A	8
Length of shortest sentence in Section B	4
Average sentence length in A (number of words divided by number of sentences)	26
Average sentence length in B (number of words divided by number of sentences)	14

2. What does your analysis of the table above show about the difference in sentence lengths between passages written in grand style and those written in common style? Say whether the statements following are true (T) or false (F).

Analysis	T	F
a. The sentence lengths in the passages are about the same.		
b. Grand sentences are nearly twice as long as common.		
c. Common sentences are nearly twice as long as grand.		
d. There is no clear pattern.		

Check through your draft and compare the length of your sentences to those in Kevin Rudd's speech. Passages written in common style should have sentences only half as long, on average, as those in the grand style. The contrast in sentence length will make those sections stand out more clearly and forcefully.

Sentence structure: repetition

The sentences in a formal speech often have elaborate patterns. This is one of the ways that speakers create the grand style that makes a speech powerful. Such patterns contrast with our everyday speech, where sentences often have simple structures.

The most noticeable feature of sentences in Kevin Rudd's speech is *repetition*. The examples below show the various types of repetition in the speech, along with their technical names.

1. *Repetition of sentence endings (antistrophe)*
   To the stolen generations, I say the following: as Prime Minister of Australia, *I am sorry.* On behalf of the government of Australia, *I am sorry.* On behalf of the parliament of Australia, *I am sorry.*

2. *Repetition of sentence openings (anaphora)*
   It is time to reconcile. *It is time* to recognise the injustices of the past. *It is time* to say sorry. *It is time* to move forward together.

3. *Repetition with addition (auxesis)*
   Decency, human decency, universal human decency, demands that the nation now step forward to right an historical wrong.

4. *Repetition by listing (parallelism)*
   That is why the parliament is today here assembled: *to deal with* this unfinished business of the nation, *to remove* a great stain from the nation's soul and, in a true spirit of reconciliation, *to open* a new chapter in the history of this great land, Australia.

Repetition in a speech serves two purposes. It *emphasises an idea* by drawing extra attention to it (1, 2 and 3 above); and it *helps the audience keep track* of long sentences and lists by making the sentence structure clear and predictable (4 above).

The key to effective repetition is to group your phrases in threes; to use identical wording and/or structures to make the repetition obvious to the listener; and to use parallel structures for emphasis.

Effective repetition: three rules
1. Group your phrases in threes.
2. Use identical wording to make the repetition obvious to the listener.
3. Use parallel structures for emphasis.

Activity 11

1. Find one more example of each type of repetition in Kevin Rudd's speech. Label each one.

2. Rewrite each of the following sentences to create the required repetition.

    a. *antistrophe* (repeated sentence endings) – emphasise the idea of *helping*

    The cataract sufferers need our help. The Indigenous Australians on dialysis need more care and assistance. So too, do the children with cystic fibrosis.

    b. *anaphora* (repeated sentence openings) – emphasise the idea of *acting*

    We must act now, because it is finally possible. We must do it, because it is finally affordable. We must, because it is ultimately right.

    c. *auxesis* (repeated word with addition) – emphasise the idea of *generosity*

    Generosity, generosity that is real, the real generosity of Australians, is what mateship is all about.

    d. *parallelism* (listing) – make the sentence clear and predictable by emphasising *change*

    We must set ourselves three goals: to make changes to the law, to adjust the attitudes of our friends and families, whose support we will need, and make the lives of those on the waiting lists better.

Go back to your draft and look for places where you can use repetition to emphasise ideas, or to make sentences easier to follow. Use at least two of the types of repetition you have studied.

You have now finished revising your draft speech.
Go to Step 4 if you want more practice in diction and sentence styles.
OR
Go straight to Step 5 on page 139 to write your final copies.

Step 4: Exercises (optional)

IN THIS SECTION:
- Practise your new skills

Do you need more practice in the writing skills you have learned? The exercises that follow will give you more preparation in diction and sentence styles. Choose the skills that you need to practise, and complete the exercises for that topic. Answers are on page 146. When you feel confident in the skills go on to Step 5 and write the final copy of your speech.

1. *Diction – grand and common styles:* Rewrite each of the following statements, changing the style as needed.

   a. *Common:* To those who kicked off this campaign, we say, "Your efforts haven't been wasted."

      Grand: ....

   b. *Common:* This is not good.

      Grand: ....

   c. *Grand:* For the victims, this is a most unwelcome development.

      Common: ....

   d. *Grand:* We must apply ourselves even more strenuously to the task.

      Common: ....

   e. *Common:* It's been a while since we last looked at these problems and tried to work out how to fix things.

      Grand: ....

   (Suggested phrases: started; began; not been in vain; not been for nothing; been too long; unacceptable; addressed ourselves to; unfortunate situation; unhappy turn of events; bad news; forge a consensus; labour more diligently; work harder; many troubled years; these grave issues; attempted to; the best course of action.)

2. *Sentences – repetition:* Rewrite each of the following sentences to create the required repetition.

    a. *anaphora* (sentence openings) – emphasise the idea of *acting as a group*

        Let us turn this page together. Together, let's grasp the opportunity. We can make a difference.

        ....

    b. *antistrophe* (sentence endings) – emphasise the idea of *pain*

        For the victims, this pain is real. For their friends and family, too, it is real. And it is real for the entire nation.

        ....

    c. *auxesis* (addition) – emphasise the idea of *fairness*

        Fairness, a spirit of fairness, on a national level, should guide our actions.

        ....

    d. *parallelism* (listing) – make the sentence clear by emphasising *vision, "know-how" and courage*

        We can build a better system if we have the vision to plan ahead, the know-how to make it work, and if we see it through with courage.

        ....

Step 5: The final copy

IN THIS SECTION:
- Put it all together
- Write the final copy
- Hand it in

Now you are ready to write the final version of your speech. Try to imitate the design and style of Kevin Rudd's speech as closely as possible. Use the summary on this page and the next to remind yourself of the steps you need to work through.

On page 141 is a checklist you or your teacher can use to assess your work.

Summary: Formula for a persuasive speech

Purpose
To persuade people to take an action or support a policy.

Ideas
- State your argument in an assertion that combines action and explanation.

- Support your assertion with proofs, including:
  - a human story (appeal to emotions)
  - facts and figures (appeal to reason)
  - statement of values (appeal to principles and ethics)

- Use pointing, linking and numbering phrases to help the audience follow your points.

- Use techniques of persuasion:
  - *apostrophe* (turning to address the present and absent)
  - *exhortation* (calling on those present to act)

Design

- Arrange your speech into five divisions:
  - introduction (address audience, announce occasion)
  - assertion (give background, state the assertion)
  - proofs (present three kinds of proof)
  - persuasion (appeal to specific groups)
  - conclusion (end with optimism and praise)

Style

- Consider aspects of ceremony and persuasion.

- Write in a grand style to create seriousness:
  - formal diction, elaborate sentences

- Write some passages in common style for contrast:
  - informal diction, shorter sentences (half the average length)

- Use correct forms of address, and emphasise pronouns (I, you, we).

- Use repetition for emphasis and clarity:
  - anaphora and antistrophe (sentence beginnings, endings)
  - auxesis (addition)
  - parallelism (sentence lists)

Assessment checklist: Project 4

Score your work as follows: 2 points for each *Yes*; 1 point for *Partly*; 0 points for each *No*. Add the scores for a mark out of 20.

Project 4: Write a persuasive speech	
Ideas	**Tick the box**
Does the speech have a clear subject? Is there a clear assertion, including elements of action and explanation?	No ☐ Partly ☐ Yes ☐
Are there three clear proofs? (e.g. a human story, facts and figures, values)	No ☐ Partly ☐ Yes ☐
Are persuasive strategies (e.g. apostrophe, exhortation) used effectively?	No ☐ Partly ☐ Yes ☐
Design	
Are the five divisions correctly developed? Does each part of the speech achieve its purpose?	No ☐ Partly ☐ Yes ☐
Have pointing, linking and numbering phrases been used to make the divisions and subdivisions clearer for a live audience?	No ☐ Partly ☐ Yes ☐
Style	
Is the speech written in a grand style to create a sense of seriousness? (e.g. formal diction, complex sentences)	No ☐ Partly ☐ Yes ☐
Are passages of common style used to help the audience bond with the speaker? Are the passages effective?	No ☐ Partly ☐ Yes ☐
Has repetition been used for emphasis and clarity? Have at least two types of repetition been used? (e.g. anaphora, antistrophe, auxesis)	No ☐ Partly ☐ Yes ☐
Does the style take account of ceremonial aspects? (e.g. correct forms of address, personal pronouns, inclusive language)	No ☐ Partly ☐ Yes ☐
Spelling and punctuation	
Are spelling and punctuation consistent and correct?	No ☐ Partly ☐ Yes ☐
Comment:	
Date:	Score:

Going further

IN THIS SECTION:
■ Get ideas for further writing

1. Collect examples of famous speeches from around the world. Some suggestions:

Elizabeth Cady Stanton:	*We now demand our right to vote* (1848)
Winston Churchill:	*We shall fight on the beaches* (1940)
Martin Luther King:	*I have a dream* (1963)
Nelson Mandela:	*An ideal for which I am prepared to die* (1964)

   Study two or three speeches, examining the ideas, design and style of each one. Make a table showing the features that all of the speeches have in common, and the features that are unique to each speech.

2. Do a close study of one famous speech, and prepare a report on your findings. Organise your report using the following categories.

Background:	Give details of the speaker, occasion and historical context.
The speech:	Comment on:
	a. ideas in the speech
	b. design of the speech
	c. style of the speech
Reception:	Describe how the speech was received, and its effects.
Evaluation:	Present your own evaluation of the speech, answering these questions:
	a. How effective is it?
	b. Would it work today?
	c. What can other speakers learn from it?

3. Write a speech imitating the design and style of one of the famous speeches you have studied.

    For variety, you might consider the following topics.

    a. Write a parody that copies the style of a famous speech, on a different topic.

    b. Translate the content from one famous speech into the style of another.

4. Choose a topic that you feel strongly about, and prepare a persuasive speech on some aspect of the topic. Before you begin, think carefully about the situation.

    a. Who is your audience?

    b. What is your relation to the audience?

    c. What will they know about the topic?

    d. Where will the speech be delivered?

    e. What outcome is expected?

    These factors will influence the style and content of your speech. Once you have a clear situation in mind, work through the stages on pages 139–140 to prepare your speech.

Quiz: Project 4

1. Name the three main types of formal speech, and briefly describe each one.

    ....

2. State two facts about Kevin Rudd.

    ....

3. Name three kinds of proof that appeal to reason, emotion and ethics. Give an example of each.

    ....

4. Describe the technique called *apostrophe*, and say why you would use it in a speech.

    ....

5. Describe the technique called *exhortation*, and say why you would use it in a speech.

    ....

6. Name the five divisions used in Kevin Rudd's speech.

    ....

7. Explain pointing, linking and numbering phrases, and say what each is used for in a speech.

    ....

8. Describe the two features of grand style and common style.

    ....

9. Name three kinds of repetition used in Kevin Rudd's speech, and describe each one.

    ....

10. State the meaning of *reconcile, rancorous* and *partisan*.

    ....

Answers for Project 4 Activities

These are suggested answers. In some cases your wording may differ slightly. If in doubt, check with your teacher.

Activity	Page	Answers
1	114–5	1. The order is 1. b, 2. a, 3. f, 4. d, 5. e, 6. g, 7. c. 2. a, b. and c. are correct. 3. & 4. Check with your teacher. 5. a.
2	116	Discuss with your teacher.
3	117–8	1. b. is the best assertion. 2. & 3. Check with your teacher.
4	119	1. This is a self-checking task. 2. a.=reason; b.=emotion; c.=ethics; d.=reason; e.=ethics.
5	120	1. This is a self-checking task. 2. a. =apostrophe; b.=exhortation; c. =apostrophe; d.=exhortation. 3. a. Let us say yes to more support for the victims of crime. b. To the victims of crime we say, "You have not been forgotten."
6	123–4	1. Check with your teacher. 2. d. and e. are pointing phrases; a, and c. are linking phrases; b. implies numbering but does not include a number. 3. a. Let me begin by first telling...; b. Second, should there still be any doubts...; c. There is a third reason for an apology as well....
7	124–7	1, 2. & 3. These are self-checking tasks.

8	129–31	1. a, b. Check with your teacher. (Sequence may differ in different speech communities.)
		2. Formal = b, d, f, g, i; Informal = a, c, e, h, j.
		3. a. Ladies and gentlemen, thank you for the invitation.
		   b. I thank you for your attention.
		   c. We have a long history of kindness to those in need.
		   d. This gathering is a turning point in our recent history.
		   e. We have a tough road ahead of us.
		4. Suggested wording: Ladies and gentlemen, it is a great pleasure to be here with you all at what I believe is a historic moment in the history of public health reform in Australia. I want to share with you today my government's plan for addressing an issue that is both a national crisis and a national disgrace. As we stand here today, thousands of our fellow Australians face an uncertain future. They are innocent victims of trauma and chronic disease, and across this great and prosperous land of ours, they are dying. They are dying not for want of money, nor for want of doctors. They are dying not for want of a hospital bed or a vial of medicine. They are dying, I am sorry to say, for want of generosity. *Our* generosity.

Activity	Page	Answers
9	132	1. This is a self-checking task.
10	134	1. This is a self-checking task. 2. b. is correct.

11	136	1. This is a self-checking task.
		2. a. The cataract sufferers need our help. The Indigenous Australians on dialysis need our help. The children with cystic fibrosis need our help.
		  b. We must act now, because it is finally possible. We must act now, because it is finally affordable. We must act now, because it is ultimately right.
		  c. Generosity, real generosity, real Australian generosity, is what mateship is all about.
		  d. We must set ourselves three goals: to change the law, to change the attitudes of our friends and families whose support we will need; and to change the lives of those on waiting lists forever.

Answers for Project 4 Exercises

These are suggested answers. In some cases your wording may differ slightly. If in doubt, check with your teacher.

Exercise title	Page	Answers
1. Diction:	137	a. To those who began this campaign we say, "Your efforts have not been in vain." b. This is unacceptable. OR This is an unfortunate situation. c. For the victims, this is bad news. d. We must work harder. e. It has been too long since we addressed ourselves to these grave issues and attempted to find a way forward.
2. Sentences – repetition:	138	a. Let us turn this page together. Let us grasp the opportunity together. Let us make a difference. b. For the victims, this pain is real. For their friends and family, this pain is real. For the entire nation, this pain is real. c. Fairness, a spirit of fairness, a national spirit of fairness, should guide our actions. d. We can build a better system if we have the vision to plan ahead, the know-how to make it work, and the courage to see it through.

Analysing style: recording sheets

Analysing style: recording sheets

A close study of style can reveal a lot about how a text is constructed and how it achieves its effects. But you must know what to look for, or your analysis will be vague and unhelpful.

Use this chart to identify specific features in the text, and record your findings. (You should also analyse some of your own pieces of work, to see how your writing differs from the work of experts, and how you might improve it.)

Diction (word choice)

Analyse a sample of about 100 words and record the following values:

Number of abstract nouns (e.g. *beauty, love, honesty, spite...*)	
Number of concrete nouns (e.g. *stone, page, rain, bread...*)	
Number of single syllable words (e.g. *eat, work, food...*)	
Number of multi-syllable words (e.g. *consume, labour, nourishment...*)	
Number of active verbs (e.g. Rain *swamped* the pavement.)	
Number of passive verbs (e.g. The pavement *was swamped* by rain.)	
Number of adjectives (e.g. *red* rose, *fair* hair, *honest* gentleman, *biggest* fish...)	
Number of technical/jargon words (e.g. *pinus radiata* for pine tree, *interface* for screen...)	
Notable emotive words or phrases (Write examples.)	

Your findings

Is the language mostly:	
concrete or abstract?	
complex (Latinate) or simple (Anglo-Saxon)?	
active or passive?	
indicative or emotive?	
general or jargon?	

Sentences

Analyse a sample of about one page and record the following values.

Total number of sentences	
Length of longest sentence	
Length of shortest sentence	
Average sentence length	
Types	
Number of simple sentences (One main clause, e.g. <u>The tall man pushed in.</u>)	
Number of compound sentences (Two or more clauses, e.g. <u>The tall man pushed in</u>; <u>the others waited.</u>)	
Number of complex sentences (Main clause with subordinate clauses, e.g. <u>The tall man pushed through</u>, hardly slowing down.)	
Forms	
Number of loose sentences (Key idea first, e.g. *Dorothy was the eventual winner, after two recounts of the vote.*)	
Number of periodic sentences (Key idea last, e.g. *After two recounts of the vote, the eventual winner was Dorothy.*)	
Variations	
Opening: main subject (e.g. <u>Josh</u> *declared his intentions.*)	
Opening: adverbial (e.g. <u>Confidently,</u> *Josh declared his intentions.*)	
Opening: conjunction (e.g. <u>After some thought,</u> *Josh declared his intentions.*)	
Opening: verbal (e.g. <u>Hoping</u> *for the best, Josh declared his intentions.*)	
Inversions – reversed order: (e.g. <u>Happy they were,</u> *when Josh declared his intentions.*)	
Articulation (linking)	
Repeated key words (Key word from one sentence repeated in the next.)	
Conjunctives (e.g. *however, also, therefore...*)	
Demonstratives (e.g. *his, that, these...*)	
Based on your findings, are the sentences: consistent or varied? simple or complex? coherent or disjointed?	

Divisions (sections or paragraphs)

Analyse a sample of two to three pages and note the following values. The first items can be counted. For the remainder, place a tick in the table to show which techniques are used.

Number of main divisions	
Number of sentences in longest division	
Number of sentences in shortest division	
Average number of sentences per division	
Methods of development	
Accumulation of detail/statement	
Use of examples or instances	
Argument or proof	
Storytelling	
Antithesis or contradiction (Taking the opposing side, or showing a contrast.)	
Transitions	
Assertion (Direct statement that advances the argument or introduces a point.)	
Repetition of word or phrase (Key words from the end of a section used to start the next.)	
Linking words/phrases (e.g. Conjunctions: *However...;* Numbering: *The second point...)*	
Announcement (e.g. *We now turn to the matter of...*)	

Figures (techniques used to arrange, develop, intensify)

These techniques (only a few of many) may be found at sentence or paragraph level, or developed through the work. Tick the techniques used in the writing you have chosen.

Arguments and proofs	
Logical chains (Arguing by steps: e.g. *"If this, then that"; assertion-example-proof-conclusion*)	
Example (Using a specific case as evidence or proof of a point.)	
Quotation (Quoting directly or indirectly from other writers; using published facts and figures.)	
Maxim (Use of common sayings or principles, e.g. *Two wrongs don't a make a right.*)	
Balance and repetition (of phrase, word, sound, idea)	
Antithesis (Linking contrasts, e.g. *"It was the best of times; it was the worst of times."*)	
Parallelism (Repetition of a word pattern, e.g. *She had the beauty of youth, the composure of adulthood, the wisdom of ripe old age.*)	
Alliteration (Repetition of consonant sounds, e.g. *The sausages spat and sizzled on the stove.*)	
Assonance (Repetition of vowel sounds within words, e.g. *surround sound*)	
Anaphora (Repetition of a sentence opening, e.g. *It woke the children. It woke the adults. It woke the dogs and the cats. It woke the entire town.*)	
Epistrophe (Repetition of a sentence ending, e.g. *The settee was white. The walls were white. The curtains were white. Even the biscuits on the gleaming plate were white.*)	
Comparisons	
Simile (A direct comparison, e.g. Obese pedestrians waddled *like ducks.*)	
Metaphor (An implied comparison, e.g. They crossed the road, *quacking and waddling.*)	
Personification (Giving life to non-living things, e.g. The wind *moaned;* the flames *leapt.*)	
Description and emphasis	
Congeries (Heaping up words, e.g. *He screamed, and cried, and wailed, and howled, and moaned, and brayed.*)	
Enargia (Vivid description appealing to the sense of sight; painting pictures with words.)	
Hyperbole (Exaggeration, over-statement, e.g. *The girls giggled. That was it. His life was over.*)	
Litotes (Understatement for effect, e.g. *He was not the most intelligent man on earth.*)	
Polyptoton (Repeating a word in different forms, e.g. The room was *hot* and the *heat* made him sleepy.)	
Other: *anadiplosis, chiasmus, parataxis and hypotaxis, polyptoton, zeugma, etc.*	

Index

Index

Index

Writing Projects 1

For more lessons in stylish composition, see *Writing Projects 1* (ISBN 9781875136292) which introduces foundation skills that prepare the student for this volume. The four projects cover a wide range of curriculum content and skills:

Epigram

■ Focus: Stylish sentences

Content: forming generalisations; writing with concise diction; writing balanced sentences (parallel, contrast, crossover).

Fable

■ Focus: Story sequence and moral

Content: creating a story through allegory and dramatisation; controlling diction through word choice; using simple mathematics to check style; adding variety to sentences through opening phrases; writing suitable dialogue.

Story

■ Focus: Realism, character and setting

Content: matching character with setting; using transitions, flashback and contrast; developing realistic detail; using detached, third-person narration; using simple, compound and complex sentences.

Review

■ Focus: Exposition, criticism, argument

Content: conveying facts and opinions through exposition, criticism and argument; constructing arguments using assertion and proof; using common divisions; expanding your critical vocabulary; using objective and subjective statements; improving sentences through expansion.

Each project features detailed analysis of a model, a rigorous study of style, and step-by-step instructions that lead the writer from plan to finished work.